RESTORE

SEEKING PEACE
THROUGH RECONCILIATION

MANAGING ANGER, CONFLICTS, AND
DIFFERENCES IN RELATIONSHIPS

A BOOK SHORT

DONALD E. JONES, PHD

J & A BOOK PUBLISHERS
www.jabookpublishers.com

ISBN-10:1-946368-05-9
ISBN-13:978-1-946368-05-8

DEDICATION

I dedicate this book to my Savior and Lord Jesus Christ. He has been with me every step of my journey upon the earth, and I so look forward to being in His presence forever and ever.

CONTENTS

ACKNOWLEDGMENTS

I want to thank my wonderful and gracious wife Carol who has supported me in this ministry with sacrifice, enthusiasm, encouragement, and accountability. Most of all, she has been a constant blessing because of her willingness to listen. I was always sharing with her the truths God had been teaching me as I studied His word and wrote this book. It consumed many hours. Thank you, Carol and I deeply love you.

I want to thank my son Gregory R. Jones for volunteering to be the primary editor of this important book. Without his time and effort in painstakingly and meticulously going over every word and every sentence checking and rechecking the sentence structure and grammar, I would not have been able to complete it. Thank you for your ministry to me. I love you my son.

I want to thank my other children, Krista, Matt, and Kara for their love for Christ and His Word and their willingness to live for Him. I love you all.

Introduction

In Matthew 14, after the feeding of the 5,000, Jesus sent His disciples by boat across the Jordan giving Himself time to disperse the crowd and find a place to pray alone. About the fourth watch of the night (3:00am - 6:00am), the boat was being battered by waves from a strong wind, and Jesus was seen by His disciples walking on the water. At first, they thought it was an apparition and screamed in fear, "It's a ghost!" Then Jesus cried out for them not to be afraid and identified Himself. Then in verse 28-29, the apostle describes Peter's bold response, "Peter answered him and said, 'Lord, if it is you, command me to come to you on the waters.' He said, 'Come!'"

So, Peter got out of the boat, walked on the water, and headed toward Jesus. Then he looked up and saw the great wind all around him. His eyes turned toward the sea, and he saw the powerful waves. Even in the presence of the Son of God, He became frightened and began to sink. He cried out for Jesus to save him. The Lord responded by immediately stretching out His hand and taking hold of him. Though the Lord could have said many things, he simply asked Peter, You of little faith why do you doubt?" Then, Jesus walked Peter on the water to the safety of the boat. Suddenly, the wind ceased, and the water was calm.

Often, we are like Peter in our relationship with Jesus. We love the Lord, and yet make mistakes, misunderstand His words and actions, and even fail to trust Him. We let the winds and torrents of our lusts and desires to get in the way of our devotion to Him. We allow the stormy seas of trouble and tribulation to make us doubt His intentions and power. We allow the flowing waters and winds of our busy lives to make us treat Jesus as an apparition and not a real person.

Yet, regardless of how far we have sunk in our stupidity, weaknesses, and rebellious sin, He always reaches His hand out to restore the relationship we have with Him. The Lord Jesus is always willing to accept our struggles, tolerate our weaknesses, and forgive our sin. He is constantly reaching out to make peace with us. At every turn, Jesus, our Father God, and His Father, and the Spirit are ready to reconcile and restore the conflicts we bring into our relationship with Him.

Here is the point of mentioning this story. God desires the same out of His children. This is found in several critical passages in the Scriptures. Two of them are mentioned by our Lord and one from the apostle Paul. All three clearly explain the truth that relationships are to be "reconciled" and "restored" to "gain back" our brother, sister, or neighbor. This is done by seeking peace through reconciliation. We should constantly seek to resolve our conflicts with people.

In Matthew 5, the Lord Jesus discusses the heart attitudes people in His kingdom should possess. After speaking of anger, the Lord presents a general principle of living in His kingdom on earth. In verses 23-24, He explains, "If therefore you are offering your gift at the altar, and there remember that your brother has anything against you, leave your gift there before the altar, and go your way. First be reconciled to your brother, and then come and offer your gift." The Greek word translated "reconciled" means "to make changes." It originates from a Greek root word that was a banking term meaning "to render accounts the same." There would be a discrepancy between two bank ledgers, and all the mistakes would have to be found and corrected in order for them to agree. We express this between people as "being on the same page." The Lord indicates that the Father desires His people to come to Him fully reconciled with each other. If we, as Christians, know that someone harbors something against

2

us, we are to take the initiative and go to them and reconcile with them. We should not wait for them to come to us. We take our responsibility and go to them. We must once again "settle accounts." They have the same responsibility.

In Matthew 18, Jesus discusses those who are sinning in the church and what all believers should do. In verse 15, the Lord commands, "If your brother sins against you, go, show him his fault between you and him alone. If he listens to you, you have gained back your brother." The Greek word translated "gain" refers "to obtaining or securing something." When a relationship is restored, we gain back everything that the other parties contributed. In this particular case, we have something against our brother, rather than the reverse. If this does happen, we are to take the initiative and confront our brother or sister to gain him or her back and restore the relationship. So, whether someone has something against us, or we have something against someone else, the procedure is essentially the same. Christians must take the initiative and reconcile with them.

The third passage involves the restoration of a sinning brother in the church. In Galatians 6, Paul opens the chapter with an explanation of how to help a sinning saint. In verse one, Paul asserts, "Brothers, even if a man is caught in some fault, you who are spiritual must restore such a one." The Greek word translated "restore" means "to render fit, sound, or complete; to mend or repair what has been broken." The word is used of a physically broken fishing net. In Mark 1:19 and Matthew 4:21, when Jesus called James and John into ministry with Him, they were in the process of "mending" their fishing nets. They were mending the holes in their net so the fish would not fall through. This restoration could easily involve a conflict between two people. Holes in their relationship need to be mended. This process involves the seeking of peace with others. Keep them in mind.

This book is a completely original work on reconciliation and resolving conflicts. It is not based on other books that I have read and simply collated. To produce this work, I carefully read through the entire New Testament verse by verse and meticulously perused the Old Testament paying particular attention to the Psalms and Proverbs. As I read, categories were built from the individual passages, rather than a set of preconceived notions brought to the various texts. These numerous categories became the individual biblical principles found in each chapter. Every passage was fully studied in its historical, grammatical, and scriptural contexts. Then, I compared my interpretations with those of past and present scholars. After this study, I have attempted to obey and follow these biblical principles in my own personal life and also utilize them in my pastoral counseling practice. I have seen the Holy Spirit use them to transform relationships of all kinds.

One last thought. At the end of each chapter, I discuss a counseling experience. Due to confidentiality, none of these are based on one particular counseling situation. Instead, I have mixed together common elements I have seen, details from books and films, bits from my own life and the lives of people I have known, and thoughts from my imagination to create a situation where the biblical principles discussed in the chapters can fully be applied. These are composites of real-life situations. Read, learn, and apply. I commend you to the Lord and His Word (Acts 20:32).

Chapter 1

Put Away Anger

In a conflict, the biggest hindrance will be our anger. This beast can rear its ugly head during any step in the conflict resolution process. It can and will destroy all the progress we might have made in a matter of minutes using just a few words. Anger is able to build a wall so high that any words or actions to restore the relationship (see Introduction) can't be heard or seen. It can spread like fire to anyone connected to the relationship. These people will usually divide up and create two great armies among family, friends, church members, co-workers, and fellow students for battle: those who take our side and those who take the other's side. The loved ones who remain neutral may be ostracized.

This displeases God the Father (1 Corinthians 1:10; 12:25). We know that God desires peace and unity (1 Thessalonians 5:13; Hebrews 12:14). Anger destroys this peace and unity in our relationships. As a result, this crazed beast of negative emotions and feelings must be managed and its expression in thoughts, words, and deeds must be eliminated. It should never be allowed to reign free and run amuck. It will spit its division producing poisonous venom on everything and everyone in its path. I use disturbing images because of its disturbing destruction. This incensed emotional monster will shatter church unity, marriage unions, parent-child bonds, friendships, and also disrupt the flow of the gospel from believers to unbelievers.

Often times, anger will actually add to the conflicts we are trying to resolve! If we are able to control our anger, we may even prevent the conflict from occurring in the first place or at least be able to resolve it quickly and efficiently. When all our angry feelings and emotions are managed, then our relationships will remain strong and save us a lot of trouble and difficulties we create for ourselves. If we are also able to prevent the expression of the other person's anger, another mess will not be made. In this chapter, we will learn how to respond to our own anger and the anger of others.

A Typical Scenario

Have you ever had or heard a conversation with a spouse, parent, or friend that went something like this? You might say, "Oh, I am so upset! It's almost family reunion time and this year I wanted to go to the cabin at the lake. For the last three years, everyone else got to pick where we went, and now it's my turn.

Then my younger brother called me and described the horrible time he had last summer at the cabin with his asthma. Apparently, the altitude is too high and the air too thin for him. He spent the entire week trying to catch his breath. Now he wants to have the reunion near a beach, where he can breathe freely. That is not what I want! So, we got into this big argument! Oh, I am so angry! What a wimp! I am telling you it is all in his head! I'm not bending this time. I want what I want for a change! He better watch out, when I get angry, there is no telling what I might do!"

The person in this scenario let his anger takeover, and evil began just as quickly. This has happened to all of us, but it is not God's way. Much of the conflicts that we experience in our relationships are due to or are intensified by anger. We get angry and want to fight it out with our words and even our fists. This ruins relationships and never builds them up. We must not get angry for the sakes of all involved.

A Scriptural Principle

This principle for resolving all conflicts will deal with the techniques needed to put all anger away thereby preventing the sinful thoughts, words, and actions that destroy people's lives. We will discuss how to respond to the anger of others in order to preserve the relationship. This brings us to the first principle which is "we must put away all anger in our relationships." Our natural feelings of anger must always be managed, but their expression in our thoughts, words, and deeds must be eliminated. This is a life-changing distinction. Angry feelings may arise, but they must not be expressed in any angry thoughts, words, or actions. There is absolutely no place in relationships where anger produces positive effects; instead, they are always negative. Though some people may consider "fighting something out" is a good idea, this never works and is not God's way. So how does the Lord desire that we handle our angry feelings when they arise?

A Biblical Explanation

Anger is one of the only emotions that God's children are not allowed to express. This is a bold statement! Allow me to explain. In Matthew 5:21-24, Jesus condemned anger as a violation of the sixth commandment. He explained that when anger and bitterness issues forth into angry thoughts, words, or any actions, these are also sins of "murder," but "murder of the heart." Paul continues to elucidate this truth. He teaches this principle simply and clearly in two different passages. In Ephesians 4:31, the apostle commands, "Let all bitterness, wrath, anger, outcry, and slander, be put away from you, with all malice." In Colossians 3:8, he then repeats, "But now you also put them all away: anger, wrath, malice, slander, and shameful speaking out of your mouth." Paul commands us to remove all our anger and wrath. The first word refers to a general anger, and the second to a quick-tempered wrath. Both are condemned.

Of course, the question arises, "What about feelings of anger, are they sinful?" In Ephesians 4:26-27, Paul answers the question. He commands, "'Be angry, and don't sin. Don't let the sun go down on your wrath, and don't give place to the devil." The Greek word translated "be angry" is the standard word for general anger. Let's take a moment for a short Greek grammar lesson. The verb "be angry" is in the present passive imperative tense. It conveys three crucial meanings. First, the verb "be angry" is in the "imperative." It means that he is giving us a command. Second, it is present tense which denotes continuous action in present time. This means that the anger does not just arise and leave as fast as it came, it could stay awhile. Third, it is in the passive voice which indicates that it has been instigated by an outside source. Something from outside the person is prompting the inward feeling. This anger is inside of us, but someone or something is provoking or stirring it up whether that is the intention or not. It comes upon us without our volition.

Those feelings of anger are not the sin. Feeling angry is not sinful; it is the manifestation of the feeling of anger in thoughts, words, and deeds that is sin. This is why Paul says, "And do not sin." When our anger is suddenly aroused, we are tempted by the flesh to express it in our thoughts, words, or deeds. The angry thoughts, words, or deeds are the sins. In the second half of the verse, Paul adds, "Don't let the sun go down on your wrath." This word "wrath" is a different word than the first one. The Greek word translated "wrath" here emphasizes the provoking of the anger. The provocation itself is in view. So, Paul is essentially saying this, "Do not let the sun go down on the provocation of that anger." Whatever instigated the anger must be dealt with by sunset. In our vernacular, we would say ASAP (as soon as possible). At the very least, some action must be taken to resolve the issue by sunset. This is the intent of Paul's words. It may take longer than a day, but we should get started. This cannot always happen because we may be unable to let the anger go long enough to really discuss it. So, the next best approach is to set up a time to resolve the issue.

This is taught in the Old Testament as well. In Psalm 37:8, David urges his readers, "Cease from anger, and forsake wrath. Don't fret." Here he uses the three Hebrew terms that designate general anger, quick tempered wrath, and hot rage respectively. Then the inspired writer commands us to cease, forsake, and don't act on them. He explains, "It leads only to evildoing." The inspired writers and our Lord all agree that anger is to be put away when it wells up inside us. Exactly how can believers put their anger away since it so easily gets out of control?

In Psalm 4:4, David provides the answer. In this dramatic psalm, David is angry. Many opponents have risen against him, and he cries out to the Lord in prayer. As he describes his anguish, he turns his attention to his future readers and explains what to do when one of God's people is angry. In Psalm 4:4, he writes, "Tremble, and do not sin; meditate upon your bed, and be still. Selah" (DEJ). Here David speaks of trembling in anger because his enemies are spreading lies about him. He is so angry that his whole body is trembling. When this feeling begins to build, what do we do with it?

First, we go to our bed. Though this may sound strange with careful consideration, it makes perfect sense. They lived in a Bedouin world of tents. Like our bedrooms of today, the room with the "bed" would be separate from the other rooms by a covering. This would be the only place someone could be alone. He does not mean to literally go to our beds but to remove ourselves from the situation which is provoking the anger. We might call it today taking a "time out." We must leave the scene of the crime, so to speak. Our bed is a quiet spot away from the provocation. It fits perfectly with Paul's injunction to "put it or take it away." We literally take the ball of fiery anger away from the situation to a restful place. The Hebrew word translated "bed" can also mean "lying down." This word conveys the idea of resting and relaxing.

Second, we must "meditate." This is not the concept of meditation we have today. The Hebrew word literally means "speak or talk." Who are we speaking to? We are talking the situation over with God through prayer and the Word. We are dealing with our anger and battling it inside us. We are recognizing that to express our anger is wrong and will not glorify God and only destroy the relationship. During this time, we should pray for wisdom (James 1:5) and search the Scripture (Psalm 119:50). It is through these that we are able to subdue our anger and renew a biblical perspective.

While we are involved in this process, David explains the final step, "be still." Stop everything else. All our thoughts, words, and actions come to a halt. Our body stops. We stop and take the necessary time to process the situation in our minds. Here too is the sense of relaxing. He is essentially saying, "Calm down." Anger must never be allowed to run rampant in our conflicts.

An Ancient Portrait

From 1 Samuel 13 to 2 Samuel 21, the Scriptures provide an example of a relationship between two men with opposite reactions to an issue between them. One refused to put away his anger and desired revenge and the other was patient and sought reconciliation. This is the story of Saul and David, the first and second kings of Israel.

The Bible indicates that an evil spirit began to torment Saul. The king's advisers suggested that a righteous man named David come and play the harp to console him and ease the anguish. This was the same David that had just been anointed by Samuel. He knew this, but they did not. In 1 Samuel 16:18, the advisers described David in these words, "Then one of the young men answered, and said, 'Behold, I have seen a son of Jesse the Bethlehemite who is skillful in playing, a mighty man of valor, a man of war, prudent in speech, and a handsome person; and Yahweh is with him.'" He was a man as distinguished as Saul himself, though not yet known by the people.

So, David was called to play music to soothe Saul's pain, whenever he was tormented. At first, Saul loved David and made him his personal armor bearer. So when Saul went out to battle, he depended on David to carry additional weapons and to protect him if needed. Then one day, a giant named Goliath appeared. You may remember the story of David facing Goliath. He came to the battlefield to feed his brothers and discovered that this arrogant monster of a human was taunting the great armies of the Lord God. Since God had delivered him on numerous occasions from lions and bears, he would face and fully defeat this arrogant warrior. With a slingshot and five smooth stones, David killed this mighty giant of a man. It was over quickly in God's power. From that day forward, Saul would not let David go back home.

Saul wanted this young warrior in his service right away. Saul's son Jonathon and David became close friends. Saul set David over his entire army, and he won battle after battle. After each of these valiant victories, the women would come outside with tambourines and other musical instruments to celebrate the victory. Now they sang, "Saul has slain his thousands, and David his ten thousands." Saul became very jealous, and his anger was aroused. In 1 Samuel 18:8-9, it is described this way, "Saul was very angry, and this saying displeased him. He said, 'They have ascribed to David ten thousands, and to me they have ascribed only thousands. What can he have more but the kingdom?' Saul watched David from that day forward."

Here is the anger that we have been discussing. Saul and David had a good relationship. Then, Saul's anger literally flipped the relationship from good to bad and soured it. Saul was filled with suspicion, displeasure, and bitterness toward him now. That victory song became a game changer. After this, the relationship with David suddenly became extremely volatile. Subsequently, the evil spirit that was tormenting Saul returned. Rather than David's music calming the king, it upset him. So, Saul grabbed a spear and threw it at David attempting to pin him against the wall. This happened twice, but David was able to escape. Saul did not want to murder David at this point but only to scare and intimidate him.

Before, Saul loved David; now he wanted nothing more than to put fear into his heart. This has happened to all of us. Someone we have a relationship with gets angry and then tries to intimidate us. The "old man" thrives on this anger and intimidation. That is why the old man has to be "put off" (Ephesians 4:22). Since Saul realized David was too well known to simply kill him, he had to devise an alternate plan. Perhaps, he could erase him from the minds and hearts of people by sending him away to the farthest outpost of his army. The people could not forget because David was still winning victory after victory. His reputation grew with each victory. This only made Saul fear him even more. Saul knew in his heart that God was prospering David in everything he did, and the entire nation loved him. This made David a real threat to his throne. Rather than dealing with his anger, he churned it (Proverbs 30:33), and let it smolder (Hosea 7:6), while he devised an evil plan to kill David.

Saul decided to offer his older daughter Merab to him if he would continue battling the Philistines. He was hoping that David would be killed in battle; then, King Saul would look innocent. David refused because he felt unworthy to marry a king's daughter, at least this one. Sometime after, the king discovered that Michal, his daughter, loved David, so he offered her to him. His anger had so blinded him that using his daughters as bargaining chips meant nothing to him. When become blinded by rage, we may not care who gets hurt in the process.

Rather than pay the usual dowry, Saul wanted David to kill one hundred Philistines. The king thought surely the Philistines will finally kill him. Instead, David took a group of men and fought those Philistines and killed two hundred of these deadly enemies. This only made Saul more afraid and fueled his anger toward David. So, David married his daughter, and Saul continually obsessed over him in anger. Eventually, it was all he cared about. The anger had finally taken over his life. The more David went out to battle, the more victories he won, and the more the people admired him. Now, it became time to get his son and his servants involved in his desire to end David's life. Since Saul knew that his son was David's closest and dearest friend, he demanded that Jonathon and his servants kill David. Anger does not concern itself with the feelings of others, even one's own children. Rather than comply with his ridiculous and wicked demand, Jonathon hid his best friend.

After several other incidences, David fled that night. So, Saul sent messengers to watch David's house, so he could put him to death in the morning. When Michal found out, the daughter of Saul quickly let him out through a window to escape. She deceived her father's men by making the bed, so it looked like David was still in it. When the messengers came, she told them he was sick. When Saul found out, he ordered them to bring the sick man to him so he could put him to death. Sometimes anger has no boundaries. The king was willing to put a sick man to death. He had also forced his daughter to decide between him and her husband. When Saul found out he had been deceived, it only added to his bitterness. Anger leads only to evil and more evil destroying every relationship in its path.

Now Saul turned the anger he had towards David and directed it to his own son. The King criticized his son and his son's mother. He accused Jonathon of choosing David over him. His son Jonathon did not realize that he was choosing David's future kingdom over the kingdom of their family. He ordered Jonathon to bring David to him so he could murder him. This finally convinced Jonathon his father was determined to kill his best friend. Jonathon now became enraged. Anger and violence often produce more anger and violence in response. Jonathon secretly met with David the next day, then they said their tearful good-byes, and he left.

While David was on the run from Saul, he wrote several psalms which were prayers and songs of worship to his Lord. As Saul kept raging against David, he was worshiping the Lord God. He did not retaliate. Why not? Saul was the Lord God's anointed king. While Saul was pursuing David, David spared his life on two occasions. Sometime after this, King Saul and his army were defeated by the Philistines, and he and Jonathon were killed in battle. The story tragically ends for Saul with David becoming king in spite of all he had done to stop him. Here the first two kings of Israel had conflict over the many victories David won not for himself, but for his Lord God which was not enough for Saul.

Notice, King Saul's anger took control and was constantly raging against David. This put in jeopardy his relationships with his son Jonathon and his daughters. David, on the other hand, practiced self-control. When he had opportunities to let the full fury of his anger unleash itself on Saul, he would not take revenge. Why? He thirsted for righteousness (Psalm 63). When we get angry, we need to restrain our lips, take a time out, meditate, and rest in the Lord. This will preserve our relationships and prevent the long road to reconciliation.

A Modern Anecdote

A widowed senior in my church made an appointment to see me so he could talk about something he had done that literally scared him to death. He told me that he could no longer trust himself to do the right thing. It started with a barking dog. This dog barked all day and all night. Because my client was retired, he was home much more than most of his neighbors, including the owner of the dog. At first, he tried to ignore it. Then he put on music to drown out the barking. After this he wore earphones whenever he was home. It wasn't long before he felt he was a captive in his own home. Then he got angry. Anger welled up in him that he had never felt before.

As the days wore on, his anger turned into a deep and dark bitterness for his neighbor and this dog. Why didn't the neighbor do anything? It wasn't long before he was done with it all. He had enough. He tried spraying it with water every time it barked, but the animal seemed to enjoy it. After weeks of this incessant noise, he finally snapped. He began to conceive of a plan to rid himself of this nuisance once and for all. He researched poisons that would kill a dog without detection. He wanted some powder that he could put into a small piece of food that the dog would quickly consume that did not have any real taste or smell. He justified his behavior by telling himself he was representing all the neighbors, and everyone would be glad the barking had stopped.

When the dog was dead, maybe the next one will be quiet and docile. Finally, he mixed the poison into the small piece of ground meat and rolled it into a ball. Then, he waited as his heart pounded for the dog to wake up from his slumber. When the dog did, he flung over the fence. As he positioned himself in a different spot in the yard to get it placed just right, he saw something in his peripheral vision. As the ball of poisoned meat lay there, he went to take a look. When he saw the big furry stray cat sitting on the fence behind his shed, shivers went up his spine. The dog had been barking at that cat! Who knows how long the cat had been there!

He suddenly came to his senses. What in the world was he doing? He turned toward the meat and saw that it was still there. He had not climbed a fence in thirty years, but there he was scaling the fence like he was eleven again. Just as he landed on the backyard lawn, the dog came running. He was so happy to see someone that he hadn't noticed the meat and began jumping up on the man trying desperately to lick his face. The man grabbed the meat and raised his hand into the air.

While the poisoned food was out of reach, he saw the dog differently than he had before. Now the man saw the dog as a pet and not a nuisance and annoyance. He found himself petting the animal. The dog calmed down and wagged his tail. When he arrived home, he contacted animal control, borrowed a cage, caught the cat, and turned the stray over to them. The barking stopped. Then he began to worry. How did he get to the place where he was about to kill someone's dog? I explained to him the power of the flesh. When it gets angry, it must be dealt with. Left unchecked, Christians are capable of doing heinous things. We began at the start of the dog's barking and looked at where he had gone wrong. He let his anger dictate what he should do, rather than the principles from God's Word. So, what does God's Word say about this situation? As soon as his anger began to come upon him, he should have taken a time-out to search the Scriptures. He needed to determine not only what to do but how to view the situation from God's perspective.

The man would have seen that he did not have a problem with the animal; instead, he had a problem with the neighbor. The Lord God's solution for problems in any and all relationships, whether the relationships are close friends or strangers, is to resolve the conflict with His principles. Instead, the man let his anger control him. We discussed how important it is to eliminate any anger that might arise for the very reason David gave. If he didn't then it would lead to every kind of "evil doing." He left committed to the fact that the next time he had a problem with his neighbor the man would follow the principles of conflict resolution while putting his anger in check. We, as Christians, must understand the wicked power of anger and how quickly and effortlessly it can take over thoughts, words, and actions.

Chapter 2

Cover in Love

Many people feel conflict is inevitable and that arguing and fighting is just a part of life, when this does not have to be the case. The Bible describes three processes that should be engaged in which prevent conflict from ever happening. People in relationships do not have to constantly quarrel and argue whenever conflict occurs. The first process has already been discussed. We should manage our angry feelings and keep them from expressing themselves in angry thoughts, words, or actions. The second and third processes deal with words and actions that instigate the conflicts. Smaller issues should be resolved by covering them over in love. Larger issues should be settled by instituting a biblical decision-making process. In this chapter, we discuss how to cover over the smaller issues in love.

A Typical Scenario

Have you ever had or even heard a conversation between a husband and wife concerning the husband's step-daughter that went something like this? You hear or say, "Honey, take a look at these craft supplies. They were left all over the table in the kitchen. I have told your daughter many times to pick up after herself. I have a presentation tomorrow morning, and she knows it is the only place in this house to prepare. I have had to take what little time I have and clean up her mess. Guess what? I am going to just throw it into her room. Yeah, I'm going to throw it all over the place, and she will have to clean it up like I did. It will serve her right! (Wife responds.) What? I know she is my stepdaughter, and I have been trying very hard to develop a relationship with her. So, you think this will ruin all my efforts with your daughter? (Wife responds.) I don't care, I am really angry! (Husband pauses and contemplates the consequences.) Wait a minute, you are so absolutely right! I can't destroy weeks of building our relationship to see it destroyed over such a small thing. What's wrong with me?"

This man flies into a frenzy about his stepdaughter and then devises a plan to repay her for leaving her stuff out. In his anger, he had chosen to destroy their relationship over a small incident. Then He begins to reflect upon it and realizes it cannot possibly be more important than the preservation of the relationship he has built with her. It certainly will not be worth the long and difficult reconciliation process it will take to restore what has taken him much time to build.

A Scriptural Principle

This scenario illustrates the fact that sometimes important relationships are destroyed over the most insignificant, often ludicrous, and even ridiculous things. In this chapter, we are going to learn how to resolve issues to prevent conflicts in the less important issues of life. Here is an important point: whether an issue producing conflict is important is up to the people in the relationship. If it can be "let go" by both parties, then it should be. If either party cannot let it go for whatever reason, it must be dealt with through the decision-making process. One partner may decide the issue is not important, and the other is being stubborn, stupid, or perhaps selfish. This attitude dismisses and undermines the respect for the other person. Often times, parties in a conflict will dismiss the other person's view because it is not their own. Our view of things is not just the only perspective that is important. This deceptive thought ruins relationships quickly. Principle two is "we must cover over the less important issues in love." Many years ago, Solomon wrote, "Hatred stirs up strife, but love covers all wrongs" (Proverbs 10:12). In 1 Peter 4:8, Peter reiterates this theme when he pens, "And above all things be earnest in your love among yourselves, for love covers a multitude of sins." These two passages which describe the same concept unveil the secret to a long-lasting relationship. We must allow our love to cover over the small annoyances, minor irritations, and even the greater transgressions that might occur as we interact in our various relationships.

A Biblical Explanation

In Matthew 5:23, the Lord Jesus stated, "If therefore you are offering your gift at the altar, and there remember that your brother has anything against you." Here He describes a typical believer who is on his way to worship the Father and suddenly remembers a fellow believer has a problem with him. What should he do? In verse 24, Jesus describes the next step, "Leave your gift there before the altar, and go your way. First be reconciled to your brother, and then come and offer your gift." Here the Lord is simply saying that God the Father does not want His children coming to worship Him when a relationship with a brother or sister is not reconciled. If an earthly father knows that his children are not getting along together, he will address their behavior first before he sees them. Why? He knows that their relationships are very important for the health and well-being of the whole family. He will refuse to see them and pretend as they are that all is well. Instead, he will help them reconcile.

The Greek word translated "reconciled" means "to make changes." It originates from a Greek root word that was a banking term meaning "to render accounts the same." There would be a discrepancy between two bank ledgers, and all the mistakes would have to be found and corrected in order for them to agree. We express this between people as "being on the same page." In our case, both of us have different renderings of the accounts in the books, and I decide that my rendering is not that crucial to the situation. So, I decide to take the other person's rendering. That is the crucial idea. It is important to notice that the verb "reconcile" is in the past tense which indicates the emphasis is on the reconciliation of the other brother with us and not the other way around. We are "to be reconciled," not to reconcile. The emphasis is on what words we need to say and what actions we need to do to reconcile with the person that has the problem with us.

Perhaps, I get into a dispute with my spouse about which route to take to a given event. I consider that getting my way on this dispute is not worth the damage it will cause to my relationship, so I simply decide to go her way. Does it really matter which way we go? Is there truly one right way? A father might be staying with his daughter, and he always forgets his key to her house. Rather than getting upset for the umpteenth time, she covers over this annoyance in love.

The first step in covering over the smaller things in love is to consider more insignificant issues briefly and overlook them. These are issues that are so miniscule or may occur so infrequently that we can immediately overlook them. They are on such a small scale that they are quickly covered over. In Proverbs 19:11, King Solomon says, "The discretion [good sense, understanding] of a man makes him slow to anger. It is his glory to overlook an offense." He explains that it is to someone's glory to overlook an offense or annoyance. This essentially means that people bring honor to themselves by overlooking transgressions against them or even the many irritations that bother them. People demonstrate exactly how honorable they are when they let sins or annoyances go.

The next step in this crucial relationship saving process is to consider some issues more carefully and cover them over in love. These are issues that are simply too big to walk by them but not big enough or important enough to demand a decision-making process. In Proverbs 10:12, Solomon writes, "Hatred stirs up strife, but love covers all wrongs." Solomon explains that when you hate someone it leads only to strife and conflict, but love can help people cover over any and all transgressions or annoyances, if they so choose. The Hebrew word for "cover" means "to cover over, conceal, or hide."

In 1 Peter 4:8, Peter draws upon this same principle when he encourages, "And above all things be earnest in your love among yourselves, for love covers a multitude of sins." Here, he alludes to Solomon's proverb. In 1 Corinthians 13:7, Paul describes love as "bearing all things." The Greek word "bear," is a synonym to this same word with an added nuance. It means "to cover, conceal, and hide with endurance." Paul, the apostle, explains that godly love might have to actually endure some transgressions and annoyances of people. Love might have to tolerate (not accept or condone) some sins.

How do we cover over something in love? The saints may reassess their commitment to the person and then decide to cover over the problem because they simply love them. We ask ourselves this simple question, "Do I love this person?" If the answer comes back in the affirmative, then we decide that this issue is not important enough to even take a chance of destroying even a small portion of what we have together. Then we let it go for the greater good of us both. We simply release the issue. In Psalm 37:8, the psalmist describes this release, "Cease from anger and forsake wrath. Don't fret, it leads to evildoing." He uses a powerful Hebrew word. The word translated "cease" means "to drop and relax." We drop the whole matter, and just let the issue go. We decide it is completely over and then relax in our decision.

Then, we abandon the issue. We walk away from it and get on with other things. The Hebrew word that is translated "forsake" means "abandon or leave behind." So, we literally walk away from the scene of the "crime" and get on with the business of living. We become busy with more important issues. Peter speaks of relaxing in the Lord. In 1 Peter 5:6-7, the apostle encourages us, "Humble yourselves therefore under the mighty hand of God, that he may exalt you in due time; casting all your worries on him, because he cares for you." The Lord will take care of everything. In Philippians 4:6-7, Paul commands us, "In nothing be anxious, but in everything, by prayer and petition with thanksgiving, let your requests be made known to God. And the peace of God, which surpasses all understanding, will guard your hearts and your thoughts in Christ Jesus."

An Ancient Portrait

A beautiful biblical example of covering over the smaller issues in love is the resolving of the issue over land between Abraham and his nephew Lot in Genesis 13. In the previous chapter, God commanded Abraham to go into the land of Canaan. The Lord was giving him and his descendants this land as an inheritance. So, Abraham left Haran, sojourned through Egypt, and landed at the Negev. By this time, he was travelling with his nephew Lot. Both of these two men were very wealthy. They had livestock, tents, possessions, silver, gold, family, servants, and hired men. Unfortunately, they had too many people and possessions to stay together without conflict and had to separate. It became obvious to Abraham that major conflict would arise between them. The number of animals they both owned were so large that the men tending them had already begun arguing and fighting over the land to feed them all. There simply was not enough room to for all that they possessed.

So Abraham took the first step in preventing any conflict. He recognized that they were brothers. This was far more important than arguing and fighting over land, water, and food for their animals. In addition, it would be dangerous to quarrel and become divided. The Canaanites and Perizzites dwelt in the land and posed a real threat to their safety. They would need protection from them. They could not afford to be battling each other over land. So, he affirmed to Lot that he saw them as brothers and did not want conflict between them. He explained that they needed to go their separate ways, so their animals could survive. Then, Abraham did an amazingly unselfish thing. He offered Lot the opportunity to choose where in the entire land he would like to go when they separated. If Lot went to the right, Abraham would go to the left. If Lot went to the left, he would go to the right.

So, Lot took him up on his offer. When Lot saw the valley of the Jordan, he chose that area. Water was everywhere, and it looked like the Garden of Eden. Moses adds that this was where Sodom and Gomorrah were located, before they were destroyed. So, Abraham settled in Canaan and his nephew settled in the valley near Sodom. Unfortunately for Lot, Sodom was an evil, immoral city. Moses calls them "exceedingly wicked." As soon as Lot had departed, God spoke to Abraham and reiterated his promise. God told him to look in every direction, and all that he could see would be owned and occupied by him and his descendants, who would be like the dust of the earth. So, Abraham dwelt at the Oaks of Mamre.

There he built an altar to the Lord God and worshiped Him. Here, we have Abraham deciding that his love for his nephew was more important than even the land that he could dwell on. Even though Lot chose the choicest land, his love for him, and the peace between them was a priority. As a result, Abraham had prevented a conflict that may have destroyed their close relationship. If he had been upset or angry about the quarreling men, he did not let it become a problem. He was patient and understanding.

Even though Lot had chosen the better land, when Lot was captured by the band of four kings, Abraham and his men rescued him (Genesis 14:1-16). Even though Lot had thought about himself first, Abraham also intervened on his behalf to rescue him from the judgment of the Lord God on Sodom and Gomorrah (Genesis 19:26-33). Abraham could have been angry and bitter over the choice Lot had made and allowed him to be killed by the four kings or the fire and brimstone. Instead, Abraham reassessed his great love for his nephew (brotherly love) decided to cover over the entire problem in love. Then, he released it, relaxed about it, and abandoned it altogether. We should do the same in all our relationships.

A Modern Anecdote

A newly married couple made an appointment with me for counseling. When I came into the lobby, they were sitting on opposite sides of the room refusing to look at each other. I went over to each one and asked them to join me in my office. They walked in one behind the other. The two chairs that they were to sit in were next to each other facing me. Each took a chair and almost in unison moved it two feet away. I asked, "So how long have you two been married?" In complete disgust, they said in perfect harmony, "Six weeks!" I asked who would like to begin and the wife responded, "Oh, please let me." She explained that the two of them dated for over a year. The courtship was romantic, exciting, extravagant, and fun. The wedding was also spectacular, and the honeymoon lavish. All was well with their world until they returned from the honeymoon.

They walked into their apartment as a married couple, and he threw his clothes on the bed. She emphasized, "He threw his clothes on the bed!" The wife asked him nicely to pick them up and put them in the hamper. He was fine with that, but he just needed a few minutes to catch the end of the game on the television. He promised he would do it as soon as it was over and flew out of the room. She shouted to him, "But I want it done now!" He mumbled something. She took the clothes and threw them in the bottom of the closet, and they were still there six weeks later. He chimed in that he hadn't needed them. Then he complained that she always forgot to put gas in the car. He could not stand the fact that every time they were on their way somewhere in her car, they had to stop and get gas.

She complained that he was terribly forgetful. He always lost his keys and had called her numerous times to bail him out. She was expected to drop everything and come home to let him in the house. He grumbled that she was always on the phone talking to someone. Whatever they did, wherever they went, the cell phone rang. She whined that he took to many long showers and always wanted the air conditioning on. This was a waste of too much water and electricity. Then her husband moaned about her clumsiness. He had never seen anyone trip and fall, walk into walls, or drop things like she did. This went on for a while longer until things became heated and then I stepped in. I sat in between the both of them and said, "Since Christ is here right now and is our Lord and Master, let's see what He thinks." They sat silent. Neither had ever considered the possibility that He was actually around and desired their marriage to honor Him. In unison, they asked, "Well, what does he think?"

I explained to them that He wanted their relationship to reflect His relationship with the church. He wanted them to love, nourish, cherish, respect, and understand each other as

He did to His church. He absolutely did not want them in constant conflict. Each person brings strengths, weaknesses, and differences to the marriage. Over several sessions, we first looked at the strengths each brought into the marriage and how they could be best utilized. We discussed some of the weaknesses of both partners and which ones could be changed and which ones could not. The ones that could not be changed would be "covered over in love." For ones that could be changed over time, we developed strategies to eliminate them. Then the many differences between them would be taken through a decision-making process and be negotiated. In essence, they should focus on their strengths, cover over the small things, and then negotiate the larger matters. I explained how important it was not to let their anger control their words and actions. The fate of a marriage should not rest on lost keys, an empty gas tank, overuse of utilities, or sheer clumsiness.

Chapter 3

Resolve in Unity

Another way in which we can prevent conflict is to take the larger, more serious issues, problems, and irritations that arise between us to a decision-making process. During this time, we decide how we will handle something together. We should set up some rules and boundaries for a particular situation and follow them whenever the circumstances may warrant. This is critical because it avoids the breakdown of a relationship through a multiplicity of small annoyances and irritations or big blow-ups and intense battles. If we utilize a decision-making process when issues come up, we can avoid many clashes which inevitably will divide us and lead to the destruction of the relationship that often took so long to build. Once a marriage commences, there are often many disagreements over a variety of issues which must be taken to this process as soon as they arise.

A Typical Scenario

Have you ever heard a conversation between a husband and wife that went something like this? He says, "Hi, Honey! I am so glad we are over that fight. I hate it when we fight. It puts this cloud over everything I do. Wow. I'm so relieved. So, I guess since we reconciled, we will buy the new truck after all." (Wife responds.) "What do you mean, you didn't agree to that? We argued over purchasing the truck and then told each other how sorry we were. I thought that meant we would get the truck? (Wife responds.) What! You thought that meant we wouldn't get the truck. Why do things always have to be your way around here? (Wife responds.) What are you talking about? I want it my way. We're done! I'm outta here! You will be lucky if I ever come back!"

The husband in this imaginary scenario thought that each of them telling the other that they were sorry about the argument solved the problem itself. This happens often. We take all the right steps to reconcile with the other person concerning an argument over an issue but actually neglect to resolve the issue itself. We fail to address the problem that started the argument in the first place. We focus on the apology for getting angry and quarreling but never resolve the issue that started it. Then when the situation arises again, and it always does, the argument resumes. We essentially pick up where we left off. Instead, we need to resolve the issue or issues through a careful decision-making process. This is best accomplished before the conflict begins. Since many issues cannot be anticipated, then it has to be dealt with as each one arises.

A Scriptural Principle

This brings us to the next principle. Principle three is "we must decide together on the larger issues in unity." This is how the foundation of relationships is laid. As each issue arises, a decision is made concerning how it will be handled from then on. Both the parties simply have to abide by the decision. This is easier said than done. Both individuals will struggle with adhering to the commitment they have made. They might have to remind each other that they made the decision together and rely on the Holy Spirit to keep them committed. At other times, both parties may decide on one course of action and discover that it will not work, so they return to the decision-making process and proceed through it again. Both must remember that relationships often last for a lifetime and require much effort to keep them strong.

A Biblical Explanation

This concept is actually implied in the word Jesus chose to use to describe the restoration process between people in Matthew 5:23-24. You may remember that Jesus declared, "If therefore you are offering your gift at the altar, and there remember that your brother has anything against you, leave your gift there before the altar, and go your way. First be reconciled to your brother, and then come and offer your gift." The Greek word which is translated "reconciled" in the English means "to make changes." The word comes from a Greek root that was a banking term which meant "to render accounts the same." There would be a discrepancy between two bank ledgers, and they would have to find the mistakes and fix them. They must do this until both ledgers match. We express this between people as "being on the same page." For us, we each have different accounts of something that happened between us, and they must be rendered the same.

In the last chapter, we decided that our rendering was not that crucial to the situation, so we took the other person's. Yet, there are times we will not be able to do that. We will desire to resolve the books. We must find the error in our thinking, calculations, or even feelings or emotions. It cannot be covered over but must be resolved. For example, we get into a dispute with our spouse about whether to purchase a particular house or not. Perhaps, we argue over whether to discipline our son by grounding him or losing the use of his car for a weekend. These might be too important to cover over. If one of the partners decides that the situation cannot be covered over, then the decision-making process begins.

The biblical decision-making process has ten basic steps. First, we must seek God's will under the Lordship of Christ. We must remember as believers that the saints do not serve themselves, they serve their Lord Jesus Christ. In Romans

31

12:11, Paul characterizes all Christians as those "not lagging in diligence; fervent in spirit; serving the Lord." We should be committed to serving the Lord in all of our relationships, not simply ourselves. As a result, both parties need to seek His will, not theirs. If both people in a relationship are believers, they both should seek God's will. If only one is a believer, then they should seek God's will in the decision.

Second, whatever decisions are made, they must be made in unity. As we approach this process, we must seek to preserve the relationship and make a decision in unity. In 1 Corinthians 1:10, Paul describes this principle, "Now I beg you, brothers, through the name of our Lord, Jesus Christ, that you all speak the same thing and that there be no divisions among you, but that you be perfected together in the same mind and in the same judgment." God desires that we find unity in our relationships among Christians whether they are our spouses, parents, children, friends, co-workers, classmates, or ministry partners.

Third, we should study the Word and pray. There should be a careful search of the Scriptures for the biblical principles that govern a particular situation. Sometimes, the Lord will speak directly to a situation with a specific principle. For example, He commands that His children should pay their bills (Proverbs 22:7; Romans 13:8), Sometimes, God does not speak directly to an issue, but He will provide governing principles which will guide them in determining His will. Though the Bible does not speak to the selection of specific spouses, it does provide several divine parameters. Spouses should be believers (1 Corinthians 7:39; 2 Corinthians 6:14), should love us God's way (1 Corinthians 13:4-8), and should be willing to fulfill their responsibilities as a husband/wife (Ephesians 5:25-33) and father/mother (Ephesians 6:1-4). If the person does not desire these things, then we should not marry such a person.

At times, the Lord will provide a general principle for an issue and leaves the specifics up to both parties to decide. An example would be Ephesians 6:4. Paul exhorts all parents to raise their children in the discipline and instruction of the Lord. They decided how to do this together. Lastly, there are some biblical principles that govern neutral activities which need righteous boundaries. Though most sports, hobbies, and artistic endeavors may be completely neutral, they can still overstep biblical grounds.

Here are several principles which govern these activities. They shouldn't make us think, say, or do impure and unholy things (1 Corinthians 6:19-20), put us in bondage as a habit we may have difficulty removing (1 Corinthians 6:12), tempt us to sin (Romans 13:10), hinder the advance of the good news (1 Corinthians 10:32-33), dishonor our God in any way (Romans 14:23), or even weaken us spiritually (1 Corinthians 10:23). While we endeavor to search His Word, we pray for the wisdom to find these principles, understand how they apply, and for the willingness and power to obey them.

Fourth, we should examine our inner motives. We should be coming to the process to follow the Lord's will, not our own selfish pleasures and desires. We should ask ourselves the question, "Am I concerned about the needs of the others involved or am I seeking my pleasure alone?" Paul, in 1 Corinthians 10:24, encourages the believers in the church with these words, "Let no one seek his own, but each one his neighbor's good." They were not decision-making for their own good but the good of the others involved.

Fifth, we should examine every detail carefully and then suggest various courses of holy action. Paul concludes his first letter to the Thessalonians with a series of injunctions. In 1 Thessalonians 5:21-22, he advises, "Examine all things, and hold firmly to that which is good. Abstain from every form of evil" (DEJ). As we plan a resolution to a problem, we need to take our time. We should systematically examine all the evidence, facts, and issues, not allowing our emotions to cloud our thinking. Then, we can rationally find a spiritual, righteous solution that would honor God.

Sixth, each of the partners in the discussion needs to listen and respond in love, respect, and understanding. These are critical. In 1 Peter 2:17, Peter sums up how we are to behave toward each other in this process, "Honor all men. Love the brotherhood. Fear God. Honor the king." We are to show one another honor, respect, and understanding.

Seventh, the parties involved should carefully assess the impact of the solutions which come to mind on everyone who is involved. We find a beautiful example of this in Acts 15, when the apostles with the saints met to discuss whether Gentiles had to become Jews first to be saved. All involved includes every person affected by their decision: children, parents, relatives, friends, and others. It even involves the yet unborn offspring of future generations.

One decision to move to another state away from family and friends will not only affect us now, but for generations to come. These new generations will grow up with their family left behind. The immediate family may be all they ever know. The change in an occupation may not only affect us, but our spouses and children. If it involves much travel or very long hours, we are not the only ones affected. Often, the feelings or future of those involved (even if unborn) are simply dismissed. This is not God's way.

Eighth, we must be willing to sacrifice and compromise for the good of all. The Christian life is not all about us. The attitude we are to have is clearly summed up in Philippians 2:3-4, "Doing nothing through rivalry or through conceit, but in humility, each counting others better than himself; each of you not just looking to his own things, but each of you also to the things of others." In Ephesians 4:2, Paul adds, "With all lowliness and humility, with patience, bearing with one another in love." In 1 Peter 5:5, the apostle Peter continues, "Likewise, you younger ones, be subject to the elder. Yes, all of you clothe yourselves with humility, to subject yourselves to one another; for 'God resists the proud but gives grace to the humble.'" All of these truths speak of the compromise and sacrifice which is directed toward others. This must be a part of the decision-making process.

Ninth, wise counsel should be sought. In Proverbs 11:14 Solomon explains it in these words, "Where there is no wise guidance, the nation falls, but in the multitude of counselors there is victory." What is the point of receiving advice from the unwise? This would refer to biblical wisdom as well as practical wisdom.

Tenth, we should continue the process until we have fully reconciled the issue. All parties must be of the same mind on the solution. This is what Paul encourages the Philippians to do with all the issues that faced them. In 1 Corinthians 1:10, describes it in this way, "Now I beg you, brothers, through the name of our Lord, Jesus Christ, that you all speak the same thing and that there be no divisions among you, but that you be perfected together in the same mind and in the same judgment."

These verses demonstrate the importance of keeping at the decision-making process until the issue is fully resolved. Once we resolve some of the important issues of conflict in the relationship, it will be much more unified and even fulfilling. Many issues in the relationships are nothing more than a series of conflicts that have never been resolved. According to Matthew five, the accounts are never settled.

An Ancient Portrait

An excellent example of how an issue should be resolved is found in a conflict between two apostles, Peter and Paul found in Galatians 2:11-16. Both were great men of God, yet came into conflict with each other. When Paul was on his first missionary journey, he founded the churches in the southern region of Galatia. They were in Pisidian Antioch (Acts 13;14-50), Iconium (Acts 13:51-14:7), Lystra (Acts 14:8-19), and Derbe (Acts 13:14-14:23). Since he was sent out from the church in Antioch (Acts 13:1-3), the apostle returned and shared all the blessings God had accomplished. Since this was mostly among the Gentiles, he was opposed by a group called the Judaizers.

These Jews claimed to be Christians and believed that a Gentile had to become a proselyte Jew first in order to be saved. Gentiles were required to be circumcised, follow all the Jewish ceremonies and dietary restrictions, and obey the Mosaic Law to become true Christians. There was such a contention between Paul and these false teachers that the church sent them to Jerusalem to have the apostles settle the matter. This instigated a meeting of what is known as the Jerusalem Council. This council included all the apostles, James, the half-brother of Jesus, and the church members in that city as well as Paul and Barnabas.

It was decided that the Gentile people did not have to be circumcised or live by the law. They did not have to become Jews first to be saved. The decision weighed heavily on Peter's testimony to the group. Peter had a divine vision in which the Lord explained that He was offering salvation through Christ without becoming a Jew first. The Judaizers refused to follow their mandate and entered the churches of Galatia that Paul established. These false teachers were only concerned about what they believed.

These false teachers criticized Paul and were challenging both his ministry and his message. Now some saints were wondering off into false doctrine and denying the person who brought them this gospel. When Peter went to visit the church, he did not follow the dietary laws of the Hebrews any longer and felt the full freedom to eat with the Gentile believers. Why? Eating kosher food only was no longer an issue. Then the Judaizers discovered what Peter was up to! They pressured the chief apostle until he succumbed and disassociated himself from all the Gentile Christians. When Paul found out, he confronted Peter.

Studying how Paul resisted Peter and how they resolved the issue without destroying their relationship will give us insight into the decision-making process. In Galatians 2:11, Paul describes the encounter, "But when Cephras [actually Peter] came to Antioch, I resisted him to his face, because he stood condemned." Note, there was confrontation face to face. The Greek word translated "resisted" means to oppose or stand against. This does not necessarily refer to an angry confrontation. So, if Paul did get angry, he had already put it away. This word refers to two people who stand against each other in complete disagreement on an issue. Did Paul and Peter argue? No. Paul investigated the situation and discovered who these people were and what they had done.

In Galatians 2:12, Paul determined this, "For before some people came from James, he ate with the Gentiles. But when they came, he drew back and separated himself, fearing those who were of the circumcision." These Judaizers had come from Jerusalem and then claimed they were following James, the Lord's half-brother. They dropped his name for credibility, though James would never have sent them. Peter had eaten with the Gentiles, then drew back and separated himself from them. This Greek word "drew back" has the idea of "shrinking back timidly." Both of the verbs are in the imperfect tense which indicates a gradual separation. Peter slowly separated himself, until someone noticed he was not eating with them anymore. The Gentile Christians thought he was being aloof because they had done something wrong. Has that ever happened to you? You get into a disagreement with people, and they start to stand aloof. They act as if you have the plague, so to speak. They make you feel that you are doing something wrong, when you are not.

It became such an issue that many others followed Peter including Barnabas. In Galatians 2:13, Paul describes it, "And the rest of the Jews joined him in his hypocrisy; so that even Barnabas was carried away with their hypocrisy." It is called "hypocrisy" by Paul. So, they knew the truth but were not following it. They were acting like hypocrites. They were not following their own beliefs. Their walk did not match their message and they were not living godly and righteously by separating themselves from the Gentiles. This had violated the very essence of the gospel.

So, the apostle asked him a question in the presence of all which is found in the second part of verse 14, "I said to Peter before them all, 'If you, being a Jew, live as the Gentiles do, and not as the Jews do, why do you compel the Gentiles to live as the Jews do?'" Wow! Paul knew Peter himself was not living by every standard of the Judaizers. Since he was not following all of their ceremonies or keeping the entire Mosaic Law, how could he attempt to make the Gentiles do it? He was a Jew living like a Gentile, and yet he wanted the Gentiles to live like Jews.

Notice, Paul reasoned with Peter by helping him examine his own actions. Then Paul gently corrects Peter. He explains to Peter that as Jews, the law could not save them, only belief in Christ could do that. Once Paul pointed this out, Peter and the other saints repented from their hypocrisy and went back to eating with the Gentile Christians. So, this conflict between these men did not lead to the destruction of their relationship but a resolution of the problem. So, let us look at the decision-making process and see how this story can illustrate it. First, the apostle Paul sought God's will under the Lordship of Christ. Second, Paul sought unity with the priority of preserving the relationship. The apostle did not argue with Peter or criticize him. Third, we can assume Paul prayed for great wisdom and sought the governing biblical principles for the situation. When he confronted Peter, he gave the governing principles that were violated. Fourth, his motives were not self-seeking or pleasure oriented. If it had been, he would not have said anything at all. Who would want to take on the chief apostle of Jesus Christ? Fifth, he examined everything carefully and then suggested a plan of action: eat again with the Gentiles.

Sixth, we assume as he listened, it was with love, respect, and understanding. There is no indication of the lack of any of these as he speaks to him. Seventh, he assessed how the decision would impact all of those involved. Eighth, though Paul might have compromised if it were another issue, but he couldn't. Why? This was divine truth, and Peter was not following the truth. Ninth, Paul had previously sought the wise advice of the Jerusalem council. Tenth, the apostle would have kept at Peter and the others until they were of the same mind. We can infer that they continued until unity was achieved. We need to follow these holy men as they follow the Lord in using the decision-making process.

A Modern Anecdote

I could hear the shouting from the lobby. My new couple had arrived for their second counseling session. They were so contentious the first session that I had to schedule them after the building had closed and the rest of the tenants were gone. Their conflict revolved around the in-laws. As is often the case, very different people marry and will bring into the relationship very different families. The husband's family was very aristocratic and proper in manners and approach. The wife's family was very down to earth and did not worry about "appropriate" ways of doing things. He was an only child, and she was the youngest of seven children.

Though they loved their son, the husband's parents were a bit aloof and not used to physical displays of love or words of affection. On the other hand, the wife's parents were all about hugs, kisses, and words of love and devotion. The husband's parents believed that the couple should make all their own decisions, and if they needed help, they could ask. The wife's parents believed that the wisdom and advice of every family member (parents and grandparents, brothers and sisters, aunts and uncles, etc.) must be utilized often. It was an insult if a major decision was made without at least consulting them.

Both the husband's parents believed in "having their own space" and not coming over uninvited. On the other hand, the wife's family believed in arriving unannounced. All were welcome at any time. Needless to say, this essentially meant that the wife's family was always around and the husband's was rarely seen. This posed a dilemma for the couple and produced a large amount of stress and conflict upon the marriage as each family sought to express their love to the couple in very different ways. The husband resented his in-law's constant interference with their affairs.

The wife resented his unwillingness to accept her family. She loved them, loved being with them, and relied on them for help. She thought his family was cold and unfeeling. The holidays became impossible for him. The husband's family believed that a holiday is celebrated on that day alone. The wife's family believed that every holiday was a weeklong event. Just the birthdays alone accounted for nine weeks of the year. How could he possibly keep this schedule up? He would have to get a second job just to purchase the gifts and supplies needed. The relationship began to feel one-sided tipping toward the wife and her family's many expectations.

Though this did take several sessions to resolve, I will provide you with the shortened version. My response was, "Let's see what the Lord says about this in His Scriptures." I took them immediately to Genesis 2:24. It reads, "Therefore a man will leave his father and his mother, and will join with his wife, and they will be one flesh."

They were now a "new family" unit. The relationships that they both had with their old families had now changed. This is God's plan. When their children grow up, then they will be leaving their old families (them) and then creating a brand-new family. This may be difficult for them to cut the "umbilical cord" and for their parents and other family members to do the same. It will be hard for them as parents when their children move on to their new families, but it is God's blueprint.

As a result, I taught them the process of decision-making discussed previously. Then they made a list of every issue that had to be decided between them concerning how they would now interact with their families and the in-laws. The goal was a decision in unity. When they had set up their new plan, they were to go as a couple and share with each "old family" individually their "new family" plan. They knew this would not be easy, but they would stay with the plan no matter what the reaction, and the Lord would do the rest. As they followed the plan, their conflicts lessoned, and their joy grew.

Chapter 4

Utilize a Mediator

There may be times where we cannot resolve a conflict or reconcile a relationship by ourselves. We may not be able to discern exactly what the conflict is, why it is occurring, or how to find a solution. The problem may be too complex, or it may simply need a fresh set of eyes to view the situation. Perhaps, both of us are desirous of finding a resolution but are too broken, upset, or hurt, to initiate the reconciliation. As these kinds of difficulties occur, it may be time to find a mediator to aid in the reconciliation and restoration process. This person should take both parties through the process.

A Typical Scenario

Have you ever had or perhaps heard a conversation like this concerning a wife and her little sister? She says to her husband, "Wow! Honey! I just finished talking to my sister, and she will not listen to me. I have tried and tried to discuss our falling out, but she will not in any way be reasonable. What? (Husband responds.) Yes, I told her it was partly my fault. I apologized for the harsh and unkind words I said to her at the last holiday celebration. She doesn't want to see me, you, or the kids. Her kids and our kids are like brothers and sisters. How can I possibly explain this to them? They will be so disappointed. I have invested so much time and effort into building our relationship, now it's going to all be thrown away. We are at an impasse. (Husband responds.) What? Really? You think that I should ask my older sister to intervene? (She pauses.) Wait! That's a great idea. She loves us both, respects our older sister, and has always valued her

43

opinion in the past. Okay, I think I will contact her by email tomorrow!" Sometimes, we have a problem with others and finally come to our wit's end in our attempt to reconcile and cannot do it. As in this simple scenario, when this occurs, it is time to seek mediation.

A Scriptural Principle

In Matthew chapters five and eighteen, the Lord Jesus commanded us to reconcile relationships with those who have something against us, or we have something against them. Unfortunately, this cannot always happen. One side may not desire it or both may not be able to figure out what went wrong or even have the skills to reconcile. When this happens, they will need some help. This brings us to the next important biblical truth. Principle four is "if there is difficulty reconciling, utilize a mediator." These mediators can assist the people involved when they get "stuck" in their problems and cannot resolve them.

A Biblical Explanation

In Galatians 6:1, Paul exhorts the Christians in Galatia to intervene in a sinning brother's life. The apostle explains it in these words, "Brothers, even if a man is caught in some fault, you who are spiritual must restore such a one." He asserts that those who are spiritual should help bring restoration to the brother. Someone else must get involved. We have seen that the "someone" could be the actual transgressor or even the one transgressed, if they turn from their sin and "become spiritual." One of them may have reconciled with God and then goes to the other to help them do the same. Though, in this context, Paul is emphasizing someone else who is doing the work. In our case, it would be a mediator.

This person (mediator) comes alongside someone and helps them repair the net of holes in their relationship with God and then the others involved. The net's holes that were created are too large or too difficult, or perhaps so numerous that the ones involved cannot mend the net themselves. They must assistance by searching for a mediator.

The apostle discusses this very concept in 1 Corinthians, chapter 6. The Christians in Corinth were suing one another in the law courts before unbelievers and Paul chastises them severely for this. In 1 Corinthians 6:5, he rebukes them and then asks, "I say this to move you to shame. Isn't there even one wise man among you who would be able to decide between his brothers?" Paul demands that believers settle their differences among themselves by finding a mediator in the church. This is what a mediator will do. They will settle the differences and help solve the problem.

So, the saints in conflict should seek a mediator if they cannot reconcile a relationship. Let us begin with the critical qualifications one must have to become a mediator. The first comes from Galatians 6:1, they need to be spiritual. This means they must be a believer and be "filled with the Spirit" when they mediate. In Acts 6:5, when a serious or dispute arose between the Hellenistic Jews and the native Jews in the serving of food, the apostles chose seven men "full of faith and the Holy Spirit." The reason for this is that someone must mediate the dispute exercising the fruits of the Spirit. Without the fruits what could really be accomplished?

The second one has just been discussed from Galatians 6:2. One must be willing to bear the burden of the situation. In Galatians 6:2, Paul states, "Bear one another's burdens, and thereby fulfill the law of Christ." This is the admonition the apostle Paul provides immediately after he exhorts them to restore the sinning brothers. They may need to help them "bear" their burdens. The Greek word translated "bear" here means "to carry off, to carry on oneself." Could this not refer to one carrying on his shoulders the restoration process with the conflicts and sins involved?

The third qualification is wisdom and discernment. They need the kind of wisdom and discernment that is capable of solving the problem in the Lord, not in some worldly way. Remember, Paul commanded the Corinthians to find a wise man among them to settle their disputes (1 Corinthians 6:5). The fourth characteristic is that mediators should have the respect of both parties in the dispute. This is actually implied in the first and third criteria. Would not selecting the wise to mediate according to 1 Corinthians 6 imply someone who would be respected?

The fifth quality is to find people who can empathize and show compassion for both sides. These mediators must help the two parties in conflict go through a difficult healing and restoration process which requires a tremendous amount of compassion and empathy. In Hebrews 2:16-17, our Lord Jesus Christ is called a sympathetic high priest who comes to our aid in times of trouble.

The sixth quality is someone who has invested something in the lives of both parties or at least in the one who has the difficulty in reconciling. This way, the mediator can make a personal appeal to one or both of the parties. This was a powerful strategy that Paul often used. In the city of Corinth, Paul had many difficulties in turning them back to God and appealed to the fact that the apostle had brought most of the believers to Christ. Paul was their real spiritual father. In 1 Corinthians 4:15, the apostle Paul reminds the church of this, "For though you have ten thousand tutors in Christ, yet not many fathers. For in Christ Jesus, I became your [spiritual] father through the Good News." So as can be seen, finding a mediator who can appeal to them in some way out of love, service, or devotion can be extremely helpful. Often, a neutral party is considered who has no relationship with either party, but neither will either party have a greater motivation to resolve the conflict.

Once we understand what kind of mediators we need, we must find them. Where can believers find mediators? The first place is in any of the "accountability" groups God has given His people for the protection of relationships. They may find them among immediate or extended members of the family (Proverbs 1:8; 2:1; 3:1, 21), church leadership (1 Peter 5:2; Hebrews 13:17), one's fellowship group (Proverbs 27:9; Romans 15:14), appropriate government authorities (1 Peter 2:13-14; 1 Timothy 2:1-4) or even grown children can mediate. This would demonstrate honor and respect toward their parents (Ephesians 6:1-2; Deuteronomy 5:16; Leviticus 19:3). A professional Christian counselor may be able to more skillfully mediate a conflict using principles from the Word (Proverbs 11:14; 12:15; 15:22; 19:20; 20:18).

Once we have found mediators who might qualify, what do they actually do? They should simply follow the biblical principles outlined in this series. They are to lead both the parties through the steps of reconciliation with God first and then reconciliation with each other. In our net analogy, they bring everyone involved to mend the holes of the fishing net together by directing the mending process.

An Ancient Portrait

A perfect portrait of discipleship is found in the apostle Paul's relationship with Onesimus whom he had brought to Christ. This is found in the letter to Philemon. When Paul arrived in Rome, he met a runaway slave named Onesimus.

After Onesimus came to Christ, Paul discovered that his owner was a dear friend of his in the city of Colossae named Philemon. For a time, both Paul and Onesimus ministered together, but it came time to return him to his master so he could face the consequences of his crime. This was a serious offense in that society.

Rather than just let Onesimus return and face it alone, he decided to use the opportunity to teach both Onesimus and Philemon some important truths concerning reconciliation, the true fellowship between followers of Christ, and obeying the law. This was a great discipleship opportunity for the both of them. Paul was the right person to do it, since he was both the spiritual father of Onesimus and Philemon. He was also an apostle of Christ, who was well respected in the church. So, Paul sent a letter on behalf of this new believer which recommended that Philemon reconcile with him and welcome him as a new brother in Christ rather than as a fugitive slave who deserved severe punishment.

The apostle begins his letter complementing Philemon on some qualities, he is now going to have to display with his newly returned slave. He lauds him for his love toward believers and his deep faith in Christ which he now wants him to show toward Onesimus. Then, Paul asserts that as an apostle he could command Philemon to embrace Onesimus but would rather entreat him as someone who loves him in Christ. He could ask him as his spiritual father; but instead, he wants to appeal to him as a prisoner of Jesus Christ.

He could appeal to Philemon's commitment to the Lord but would rather implore him as someone who himself has made many sacrifices for the Lord. Philemon needs to do the same in this difficult circumstance. Paul asserts that God really had a purpose in this slave running away, and it was for his salvation. Philemon has Onesimus back as a beloved brother in the flesh and the Lord. He is especially a beloved brother to Paul. Rather than punishing his new brother as a slave, he should be embraced. Then Paul mentions that the slave may have owed him money probably either through theft or through the money lost in his absence of service so he would pay for it. Though Philemon could have afforded it, Paul did not want the loss of his friendship. He speaks of the joy and refreshment of his heart he is going to feel when he learns what Philemon has done.

His joy and refreshment will result from Philemon not only obeying but even going beyond his many suggestions. Then he indicates that he would be coming for a personal visit, so Philemon would face the apostle himself. This will definitely encourage Philemon to do what was needed to be done. His companions also greeted him.

This will encourage his right actions because they will know of Philemon's treatment of Onesimus also. There were several: Epaphras, Mark, Demas, and Luke. These were his fellow workers and mighty men of faith. Two of these men, Mark and Luke, wrote New Testament gospels. Though we are not told specifically what happened, we can be assured that Philemon welcomed Onesimus into his own household and church at Colossae. There is no indication anywhere in the Bible that Paul had to mediate the situation again.

Perhaps, once Paul's letter was read, Philemon did the unthinkable to the unbelieving Roman world, he unchained and released Onesimus. Then this Roman master, Philemon, reached out his hands and cried, "Welcome, my brother!" Here, the apostle Paul demonstrates, for not only Onesimus and Philemon but all Christians, exactly how a mediator mends the broken net of a relationship between two saints. Once resolved, this conflict should not appear again. If it does, the process may be used again to resolve the conflict.

A Modern Anecdote

There are numerous people who are involved in various kinds of ministries in the church. This can be such a blessed time when we constantly put the Lord Jesus first and desire to humbly serve and glorify Him. Unfortunately, after we come to Christ, we are still human and have a flesh that constantly entices us to desire things our way only, even in ministry. One day, I received a phone call from a pastor who had two dear Christian ladies in his office who were in charge of the new mom's ministry in the church. They both loved the Lord but were from two different generations with different personalities. The younger one (middle twenties) was a bit of a free spirit, very creative, and a people person. The other one was an older woman (senior years), who had managed various ministries in several churches was serious, focused, always functioned with proper planning, and was more task oriented. Their pastor asked the two women to work together.

This would follow Paul's injunction encouraging the older women in the church to teach the younger women. The younger woman was a brand-new mom who made up for her inexperience with great enthusiasm and high energy. The older woman had raised five children, now had twelve grandchildren, and even two great grandchildren. She was experienced and capable but moved slowly and precisely. From the first day in service together, the two women had clashed. The younger woman really wanted to start calling moms about the new ministry, and the older wanted to take some time and design a flyer to put in the bulletin. The younger wanted a simple time of prayer, bible study, and fun. The older desired to train the new moms systematically on every aspect of motherhood and child development. The younger woman wanted to have the moms host the weekly meetings in their homes so all could be a part of it. The older

RESTORE - A BOOK SHORT

woman felt that it should be in the church nursery where it was safe and secure. Every single suggestion one made was countered by the other with the opposite. Then, they came to a standstill.

They were driving each other crazy and had not yet had one meeting with the new moms. The word got out that these two were having so many difficulties that none of the moms wanted to attend because of the conflict. The pastor realized that those ladies needed a mediator. They agreed to see me if I would come to his office, and the church could pick up the cost. I asked the pastor if he could sit in on the counseling as we dealt with these two ladies that were having so much difficulty. When I arrived, I had each lady tell me her side of the issue. Once this was provided, which I just described, I explained to them that in every relationship, the parties bring into it many strengths, weaknesses, and differences.

Their strengths need to be embraced and the weaknesses should be eliminated if possible or planned for when not, and the differences must be negotiated. Then I taught them the decision-making process found in this chapter. We made a list of their strengths that they brought and divided up the various tasks according to those strengths and their other abilities and gifts. We discussed some of their weaknesses and created a plan for each supporting the other, if needed. For example, a signal would be used when the younger woman was speaking too long and beginning to go off the planned program during the meeting.

Another signal would be given if the older woman began to be rigid and did not allow something spontaneous to occur. Then, we negotiated the differences between them in their views of what was still left to be done. This negotiation took some time, and there was compromise on both sides.

Lastly, we discussed the critical biblical principles dealing with unity and making Christ Master and Lord of ministry, rather than either of them. After their mediation, we prayed together, and a new mom ministry was launched.

Chapter 5

Refuse and Suffer

There may be a time in our lives where we simply refuse to reconcile with others. We might be angry and bitter about what they did to us or our loved ones and decide, regardless of what the Scriptures say, we will not do it. We refuse to make peace with them. We will not cover over their sins in love or go to a decision-making process. When this occurs, our Father, as a loving Father, steps in and will train us to follow His blueprint. The Lord Almighty will not allow His children to be in a state of constant conflict and strife. If we, as Christians, refuse to reconcile our relationships with others, then we, as God's children, could suffer the discipline and consequences of the Lord.

A Typical Scenario

Perhaps, you have had or heard a conversation between a grown child and his or her father that went something like this? The phone is answered and you say or hear, "Hello? Hi, dad what's up? (The dad responds.) What do you mean you can't make Natalie's recital? She is your only granddaughter! Since you missed all my activities, don't you think that you could make my daughter's recital? (The dad responds.) Oh, I understand alright! Well, I refuse to understand! I have spent my whole life hearing all your excuses. I could have written a book listing them all in detail.

There have been so many over the years. Look Father, we are finished! You will never ever come to another event that involves Natalie. In fact, you will be lucky if you ever see her or even me again! Goodbye for good and please do not ever call me or anyone in my family ever!"

Sometimes, people will cause us to become angry, bitter, or upset as in this scenario. This might result in our refusal to resolve an issue. Rather than deal with the problem and reconcile a relationship, we shun, rebuff, gossip, backbite, or even cut the person off altogether. Unfortunately, this may also discontinue all the relationships that may be connected to that one, such as Natalie, who was the granddaughter in our scenario. She did nothing wrong and now cannot see her grandfather again.

A Scriptural Principle

In this chapter, we discuss a principle that deals with the many consequences that proceed from a refusal to reconcile a relationship. Before we decide to end or refuse to restore a relationship, we must understand the ramifications of this decision to us and all others. Principle five is "if we refuse to reconcile, we will suffer the adverse consequences." This is not necessarily easy. Not all commands can be immediately obeyed sometimes there may be an inner struggle within our hearts to follow God. Why? To restore a relationship is truly a divine act, not a human one. To act divinely requires real divine thinking and divine power. Our broken relationships must be viewed divinely to act differently.

A Biblical Explanation

Why would God make His children suffer if we will not reconcile with others? Why is getting along with people so important to Him? The answer is found in His own divine character. We cannot refuse to reconcile relationships with all people because God is a God of peace (2 Corinthians 13:11; Romans 15:33). Therefore, His divine blueprint for relationships is the establishment of peace among people. He desires peace between Himself and others. He desires peace among His children and between His children and the world (those who are unsaved).

In Mark 9:50, Jesus Christ, the Prince of Peace, declared, "Be at peace with one another." If believers will not reconcile, conflict occurs, not peace. In Hebrews 12:14, the author says this, "Follow after peace with all men." Paul, in 1 Corinthians 13:11, Paul asserts that we are to "live in peace." God desires His children to live in peace. When His people continue to refuse to follow His blueprint of reconciliation, the Lord will intervene, and we will suffer the consequences.

The first consequence is direct discipline from God. As we live our Christian lives on earth, we should grow more and more like our Father in heaven and into the image of His Son Jesus Christ through the power of the Spirit. In 2 Corinthians 3:18, the apostle Paul explained that all Christians are being "transformed into the same image from glory to glory, even as from the Lord, the Spirit." Christlikeness is the goal of our Christian lives. In fact, the purpose of the Lord's church is to conform all believers "to the stature of the fullness of Christ" (Ephesians 4:13).

When we are unwilling to conform to Christ's stature in reconciliation and restoration of relationships, our Father will provide some assistance through His discipline and training process. If we will not be at peace, just as God is at peace, then He will compel us as His children through His discipline. This is taught in Hebrews 12:4-11. God as a loving Father disciplines His children to be righteous just like a human father does. A father spends time teaching his kids to get along and work things out among themselves and with their siblings. This is God's sharing and peace process and is a fundamental practice God teaches His children.

The second consequence for refusing to reconcile could come from the church. Not only can the Lord intervene directly, but He can also work through His local church. In Matthew 18:15-16, the Lord Jesus Christ explained what to do if someone has sinned against us. We must go and gently confront him. If he listens to us, we gained back our brother.

If they refuse to repent and reconcile, we are to take two or three witnesses to confront the other person. These are not people that we told about the offense but people who had witnessed the offense. The witnesses can help with that. If the person still refuses to repent and reconcile, then we take it to the local church. Once the church has determined that there is unrepentant sin occurring, they will begin the final step of discipline. This is God's method of instigating and encouraging someone to reconcile.

The third consequence or act of suffering may come from the government if we have broken any laws (violence, abuse, etc.) or need legal assistance (separation, divorce, etc.). The apostles clearly describe the government as an instrument of God. It was placed into power by the Lord and may become involved if the conflict escalates or it cannot be resolved. In 1 Peter 2:13-14, Peter writes, "Therefore subject yourselves to every ordinance of man for the Lord's sake: whether to the king, as supreme; or to governors, as sent by him." We are to submit to the governing authorities. Why? Peter continues, "For vengeance on evildoers and for praise to those who do well." They are to punish evil and praise good. If we refuse to reconcile and the conflict intensifies, the police may come.

The fourth consequence that may occur when we refuse to forgive and reconcile may be the terrible inner anguish that comes from a broken heart, anger, bitterness, despair, fear, or grief. People can experience extreme emotions and feelings when relationships begin to disintegrate. They have invested so much, and there is so much to lose.

In Psalm 32, which must have been a similar occasion, this repentant king David compared the inner torture from his transgressions with the inner agony of a physical crushing of the body. In Psalm 32:3, he remembered, "When I kept silence, my bones wasted away through my groaning all day long." Refusing to repent of his sin caused a deep groaning within him as if his very bones were wasting away inside his frail body.

In verse 4, he continues, "For day and night your hand was heavy on me." He depicts God as pressing His divine hand upon him day and night until it was too great to bear. He closes the verse with these words, "My strength was sapped in the heat of summer." God's divine hand weighed so heavily upon him that it sapped him of his strength in the same way the sun does in the heat of summer. Jerusalem can easily go to triple digits. This causes one to become feeble and debilitated. Our suffering can also go to the triple digit mark as it widens and deepens when someone refuses to mend a broken relationship with us.

The fifth consequence for refusing to reconcile may be the heartache from watching the pain and suffering brought to the innocent individuals, especially children, who may love the person, who is despised and hated. This occurs often in the bitterness among relatives (spouse, parent, child, aunt, uncle, grandma, and grandpa, etc.). If we are in conflict with our relatives, then no matter how angry, bitter, disgusted, or deeply hurt we may feel, these people will always be family members. Regarding divorce that person will always be the mother or father of our children.

An Ancient Portrait

The Old Testament provides an enlightening example of bitterness, anger, and grudge bearing that led eventually to violence between two half-brothers and a sister. In 2 Samuel 13 the story is told of Absalom, Amnon, and Tamar. King David had several wives who had children. Absalom, one of David's sons, had a beautiful sister named Tamar. Amnon, one of Absalom's half-brothers, fell in love with her. In fact, Amnon was so in love and in lust with her that he became frustrated and made himself ill.

He wanted to sleep with her, but she was a virgin and desired to keep the marriage bed pure and sacred. Amnon had a sneaky, crafty, conniving cousin who decided to help him in his lustful frustration. His name was Jonadab. He asked his cousin, addressing him as "O Son of the King," why he looked so depressed. Amnon told him that he was disheartened because he wanted his half-sister, Tamar. So Jonadab conjured up a plan to solve the problem.

He suggested that this son of the king pretend to be sick, and when his father, David, came to visit him, he should ask if Tamar could bring him some food to eat. Perhaps, she could even prepare it right in front of him, so Amnon might watch. Then as his sweet, naive sister served and comforted him in his affliction, Amnon would take her. This was forbidden by God. In Leviticus 11:9, He says, "You shall not uncover the nakedness of your sister, the daughter of your father, or the daughter of your mother, whether born at home, or born abroad."

Then in Leviticus 18:11 God also states, "You shall not uncover the nakedness of your father's wife's daughter, conceived by your father, since she is your sister." Later in Deuteronomy 27:22, Moses reiterates this commandment,

58

"Cursed is he who lies with his sister, his father's daughter or his mother's daughter. All the people shall say, 'Amen.'" So, they both knew that what Jonadab had suggested was a terrible transgression and sin.

Yet, Amnon put the plan into action. David, who should have been much more discerning, bought the whole act and summoned Tamar. According to the customs at the time, any unmarried daughter was usually kept in seclusion from men so that no one could see them alone and be tempted. David did not follow this custom and asked her to make some cakes in Amnon's presence and feed her brother to assist him in his weakened state. She did not protest at all because she trusted her half-brother to respect her virginity. When Amnon feigned his sickness, Tamar came to wait on him. Perhaps, she thought that she was his angel of mercy; instead, she was about to become a victim of rape. So, Tamar traveled to Amnon's house. In front of him, she took the dough, then kneaded it, and made cakes for him. Amnon watched her prepare the cakes while burning with desire for her. Finally, when the whole process was over, she set the cakes before him, innocently expecting him to eat.

Immediately, Amnon refused to eat, and he sent everyone out of the house. Then, he told her to bring the food into the bedroom and asked her to feed him from her hand while he lied down. When she reached over to him with the cake, he grabbed her hand and demanded, "My sister, come, lie with me." He addressed her as a sibling, rather than as a woman. This demonstrated the extent of his evil perversion. Tamar refused and begged him not to violate her. She entreated him not to take away her most valued possession. This would be disgraceful in the nation of Israel. Amnon would be disgraced because he had raped her. His sister would be disgraced because she would lose her virginity and would be considered unholy and defiled. Their family would be disgraced because this shameful thing was never ever done. Tamar explained that she would never rid herself of this humiliating reputation, and Amnon would be considered a complete fool among his people. She implored him to simply speak to their father, and he would let them marry properly.

However, as lust filled his heart and body, he refused to wait. Since he was much stronger than her, he forced himself on her and violated her. Once the deed was done, his lustful, loving feelings immediately turned to disgust and hate for her. The author says that his hate was even greater than his love had been. When he was done with her, he screamed at her to get out! He was such a hypocrite that though he was the one who violated her against her will, he now saw her as defiled and dirty. Then she pleaded with him to let her stay, sending her away was even worse than violating her. People would think that she had instigated this shameful act. She begged him to marry her and end this embarrassment. Since she would not leave, he had several of his servants throw her out and lock the door. How utterly humiliating! She was the daughter of the king of Israel. The virgin daughters of the king would wear long-sleeved garments to signify their virginity and wholesomeness. When this happened, she tore her long sleeves off and put ashes on her head. She put her hand on her head in shame and went away crying aloud in humiliation.

She went right into the arms of her brother Absalom. He knew right away what had happened. He asked her if she had been violated by Amnon. When she told him that she had, Absalom asked her to remain silent because he would handle it in his own way. Her brother explained that her silence would be the way to keep this terrible atrocity within the confines of their family. Obviously, he reasoned in his mind, "If a family member did the harm, then it would take another family member to get revenge." His sister remained

RESTORE - A BOOK SHORT

"desolate" in Absalom's house the rest of her life. This meant she would never ever marry. This was a great tragedy!

Eventually, her father, King David heard about what happened. The Scriptures indicate that he got angry. That's all. There was absolutely no fatherly discipline or even any legal ramifications for this horrendous act. Nothing! After this, Absalom hated his half-brother and did not speak to Amnon for two years. For two years he let the bitterness well up inside him, until finally the moment of revenge came. It was the time of the year when the sheep were sheared, and the owners of the sheep would have a feast. So, Absalom invited all his half-brothers (the sons of the king) to a sheep shearing feast.

First, he invited his father and all his servants, knowing his father David would refuse to come. Yet, he kept insisting which would soften David's heart toward his plight of not being able to celebrate with his family members. In this way, his real plan could go into effect. So, he asked his father if he could invite all his brothers (blood and half). He wanted Amnon but the pretense required that all his brothers come. He specifically mentioned Amnon's name.

King David was not the least bit suspicious, even though Absalom had not spoken to Amnon in two years. Did David not know that? Nevertheless, David agreed and blessed him. Then, Absalom left. As soon as he arrived home, Absalom commanded his servants to strike Amnon when he became drunk at the celebration. Though they protested, He told them not to be fearful, even though they were striking the king's son. He would simply say they were obeying him. He desired all the revenge and would take all the blame. He encouraged them to be bold and courageous as they killed him! So, his servants prepared themselves. During the party, Amnon became intoxicated, and they murdered him.

Then their other brothers immediately fled. So, Absalom killed his brother through others, as his own father David killed Uriah through others. When the other brothers were on the road home, David falsely received word that all of his sons had been killed by Absalom. He tore his garments and lay upon the ground in mourning. Of course, Absalom had to flee. When David's watchman saw the other sons coming, he informed David. When they were all reunited, the king and his sons wept bitterly for Amnon.

Absalom headed to his other family for safety. He found protection with Talmia the son of Ammihud, his maternal grandfather, who was the king of Geshur (2 Samuel 3:3). According to Numbers 35:21, Absalom deserved the death penalty for pre-meditated murder. As a result, he needed the protection of a king and army. David mourned for his son every day. Absalom stayed there three years. David's heart was broken over Absalom and was comforted concerning Amnon because he was dead.

What happened next was a terrible tragedy. Absalom was so angry because David refused to see him, he took over the kingdom from his father! But that is for another study. The point is that Amnon did do a despicable deed and deserved the full weight of the law on his shoulders. Absalom refused to reconcile with him and let his jealousy and anger churn for two long years while he bore a bitter grudge and spent much time plotting his revenge on his half-brother.

What a terrible situation everyone was in. The ultimate result was the division of David's family, David losing his kingdom to Absalom, and then Amnon and Absalom losing their lives in death. We need to reconcile our relationships with others and not allow the flesh to become angry and bitter which causes multiple problems for ourselves and the others. We cannot refuse to reconcile.

A Modern Anecdote

Often times, a congregation of believers see their pastor upfront on Sunday mornings with a smile on his face and the joy of the Lord in his heart which is simply contagious. Yet, they are not immune from the disappointments of life and sometimes responding in a less than God honoring way. One such pastor came to my office to discuss his relationship with a fellow pastor in a city some fifty miles away. He was the pastor of a small church who was struggling with their finances and attendance and needed to make a dramatic move. His pastor friend had a large congregation and was well known, admired, and respected throughout the state. The pastor of the small church decided to ask his friend to come and do a weeklong series of messages on marriage which would attract a large crowd. The entire congregation was thrilled.

There were months of preparation. Almost everyone in the church became involved. A larger stage was planned and built by hand. The church band recruited members from nearby churches and practiced relentlessly. Many purchased and prepared large amounts of refreshments to serve the numerous guests. Brochures were carefully prepared, and gospel booklets purchased. When the offerings were not enough to cover the expenses, the church took out a small loan. As the day grew nearer, the anticipation grew. The church bought ads in the local paper, put up numerous flyers around their small town, and posted on as many social media sites as they could.

A room was reserved for the pastor at the best hotel in town so he could have the privacy needed to prepare. The whole town was talking about the arrival of this famous pastor and the other pastor's church. The Wednesday before his Sunday arrival, the pastor cancelled. He sent his friend an email stating he had made too many other commitments and had to cut back. The small church pastor was completely devastated. Repeatedly, he attempted to contact his friend but to no avail. The church secretary told him that the pastor had traveled out of town, and he could not be reached. Unfortunately, the event had to be cancelled, and the people were broken-hearted. When he explained the cancelation at an emergency church meeting the next night, deep inside him came an anger and bitterness that he had never felt.

He could not understand how a friend, who was closer than a brother, could do such a thing. They had known each other since childhood, were best friends throughout school, played city league baseball, and attended the same college and seminary. In response to his feelings, he sent the ex-friend a scathing email. What they had in this temporal life on earth was over, but he would see him eternally in heaven. He knew this was wrong, but he was so conflicted that he came to me for advice.

I explained to him all the principles from the Scriptures in this book. Then, I implored him to reconcile with his brother. With that, he stood up, said he would let me know, and left the room. When he returned the following week, he was even more bitter and disturbed. He told me that the more he thought about it, the more he grew in his resolve not to restore the relationship. Once in a while, I may encounter a stubborn heart and then do my best to be understanding.

Yet, when we choose to disobey the commands of the Father and decide to follow our own bitter hearts, I must issue a stern warning. So, I discussed with him the all the truths in this chapter and warned him that God disciplines His children. If he refused to follow God's mandate, he would suffer the consequences. Many weeks went by before I heard from him.

After three months, I received a call from the pastor. He told me that his raging anger and deep bitterness began to affect all his relationships. The church leaders were split on what to do with him. His wife was pulling away, and his children were wondering what was wrong with their dad. Everything was going against him.

Slowly, he began to realize that he was simply receiving the consequences from his own sinful attitude. God was unhappy with Him and wanted him to reconcile with his friend. So, he did, and the relationship was restored between the two. He told me that his friend was coming to do a week long conference and his church would take care of all the bills. What a blessing! He thanked me for my advice from the Word and my patience with the process he had to go through. All was well again.

Chapter 6

Love the Obstinate

Sometimes, no matter what we do to resolve the conflict, people choose to stand against us or end the relationship. What do we do then? We may see them at gatherings of friends or a family event, how do we treat them? When they refuse to reconcile and choose to be obstinate, we must love them anyway. Our response to their obstinacy is not based upon their response to us; instead, it is based upon God and what He desires. When we find ourselves suddenly in a conflict or stalemate, we can take our eyes off the Lord, and put them squarely upon the other person. This change in perspective almost certainly will lead to nothing but mutual retaliation making the problem worse. Whether they decide to reconcile with us or not, our God desires that we still love them through words and actions.

A Typical Scenario

Have you ever had or perhaps heard a conversation that a husband had with his wife concerning their daughter that went something like this: He says, "Hi Honey! Well, I called our daughter three times, and she won't answer. Her brother is getting married; you would think she would want to come to his wedding? This is all messed up. This estrangement is going to tear the family apart. If she keeps this up, she will never meet her sister-in-law or see many of her future nieces and nephews. (Wife responds.) What? Exactly, we won't be able to go to her wedding, meet our son-in-law, and ever see our future grandchildren. Doesn't she realize this is going to affect generations of our families and all the other families involved for many years to come? What? (Wife responds.) Yes, I have tried everything to reconcile. She simply won't respond. It has been five years already! There is nothing else I can do!" Here the father has taken all the right steps to reconcile with his daughter, but she will not respond.

A Scriptural Principle

In a perfect world, when we have proceeded through the steps we have discussed so far, the relationship is restored. All is well with the world. Most of the time, in our imperfect world, the relationship is still restored. At other times, it is not. Sometimes people become obstinate and are unwilling to restore the relationship. In this chapter, we will study how we are to exactly respond to them. If they choose to be bitter, angry, or bear a grudge, what do we do? If they decide to hate, criticize, or even get revenge, how do we react? If the relationship is not only ended but they begin acting like a bitter enemy, how should we respond to them? The answer is found in the next biblical principle. So, principle six is "if someone refuses to reconcile, we must love them anyway."

A Biblical Explanation

When people refuse to reconcile with us, our flesh wants to respond in like manner. It is called "retaliation." If they hate us, we will hate them. If they ignore us, we will ignore them. If they criticize us, we will criticize them. If they take revenge, we will take revenge. Unfortunately, this leads to a spiral downward into every kind of evil. David asserts in Psalm 37:8 "Cease from anger, and forsake wrath. Don't fret, it leads only to evildoing." Retaliation and revenge lead to utter devastation. It destroys relationships, ravages families, ruins friendships, and can split churches in half. This is not God's way. Paul explains God's way in 1 Thessalonians 5:15, "See that no one returns evil for evil to anyone, but always follow after that which is good, for one another, and for all." So, when people harm us, we are not to seek their harm in return. Instead, we are to seek their good. Paul reiterates this concept in Romans 13:19-21.

So, people refuse to reconcile even after our best efforts what do we do? First, if given the chance, we should show them love. Jesus states in Matthew 5:44 and Luke 6:27 that Christians are to love their enemies. The word "love" in this passage has nothing to do with romance but something much deeper. The Greek word essentially means to value or prize someone or something. This word was utilized by Jesus and His disciples to speak of valuing to the point of sacrifice. The classic use of the word is in John 3:16, where Jesus asserts that God so loved the world that He gave His Son. God so valued the world that He gave even though it was hostile to Him.

So, if they come to us with important needs to be met, we should value them and make the sacrifice. Though, we have two constraints on our love as Christians: we must love in knowledge and discernment. This means we are to know the situation fully and know the biblical principles that govern that situation; then, we must discern the best way to love the person. In Philippians 1:9, Paul declares, "This I pray, that your love may abound yet more and more in knowledge and all discernment." If we have an estranged family member who has a gambling problem, it would not be prudent to give them cash to meet their need.

Second, if given the chance, we should give a blessing to them. Not only are Christians to love their enemies but bless them. In the two passages of Matthew 5:44 and Luke 6:28,

Christians are commanded to bless those who curse them. Blessing someone was a very familiar Old Testament idea. A typical blessing is found in Ruth 2:3-5. Here, Boaz arrives at his fields and greets his reapers with "May the Lord be with you," and they return with "May the Lord bless you." This general blessing was full of meaning. These words expressed a genuine and heartfelt desire that the other person would find protection and safety in God.

This blessing is in contrast to cursing them. Paul speaks of this kind of blessing that should be made upon the enemies of Christians. In Romans 12:14, Paul commands, "Bless those who persecute you; bless, and don't curse." God's children should wish His blessing upon their persecutors or enemies, both in their hearts and from their mouths. Obviously, God's ultimate blessing would be in their own repentance from their evil responses to our attempts at reconciliation and the salvation of their souls.

Third, if given the chance, we should do good to them. Not only are Christians to love and bless their enemies, they are to "do good" to them. In Matthew 5:44 and Luke 6:27, believers are commanded by the Lord Jesus to do good to those who hate them. When believers are seeking to do good works for the glory of God, they must look to their enemies. In our case, those who are estranged can become recipients of our righteous deeds.

In verse 16 of the same chapter, the Lord Jesus proclaimed these words, "Even so, let your light shine before men; that they may see your good works, and glorify your Father who is in Heaven." We must let our lights shine before the world. When others refuse to reconcile with us and we treat them well, this doing of good towards them shines our light in their faces. It demonstrates that we are much more like our heavenly Father who is in heaven.

Fourth, we should pray for those who refuse to reconcile with us. In Matthew 5:44 and Luke 6:28, Christians are told to pray for those who mistreat them. What do we pray for? If they are unbelievers, we should pray for their salvation and God would help us restore the relationship with them. We should entreat the Lord to use our good deeds toward them to build a bridge or at least bring them to Christ. Paul and the other apostles witnessed many people receive Jesus as Savior and Lord who had previously opposed them. We should pray that God would open their eyes so they might become believers in Him and even proclaimers of the gospel.

In Acts 16:35-41, the jailor who opposed Paul came to Christ through Paul's demonstration of love (not escaping). In Acts 18:1-11, Paul was thrown out of the synagogue; yet later the synagogue leader and all those in his household came to Christ. If those estranged to us are believers, then we should pray that God would open their hearts to us. We should ask God to convict those who will not reconcile of their sin. Of course, we should always keep in mind that we ourselves could have easily been in their place.

Fifth, if given the chance, we should be unwilling to resist them in time of need; instead, we should go out of our way to meet them. In Matthew 5:39-41 and Luke 6:29-30, the Lord Jesus declared that His followers should not resist their enemies. The Greek word which is translated "resist" means "to oppose or stand against." A careful reading of the context demonstrates that it involves dealing with enemies in need. In Matthew 5:42, after giving three examples of not resisting enemies, Jesus proclaimed a truth or principle to guide our interactions with people in general and especially those who oppose us. We are to give to anyone who asks or wants to borrow from us. We are to act like our Lord God who sends sunshine and rain upon evil as well as good people. We can never forget this important truth!

Christians will go out of their way, beyond their comfort zone to meet the needs of people, even the obstinate or their enemies. Do others need something believers have and then humiliate them to get it? There is no need to challenge them, the obstinate can have it. Do others sue believers because they need something those saints may be wearing? They do not need to bother, they will give two articles of clothing to these people, enemies or not. Do others need the saints to help them carry something a long distance? There will be no problem, they will be glad to carry it twice as far. As God's children, we are not like other people even our enemies will be helped. We will respond with love and allow our God to respond with justice.

An Ancient Portrait

A good illustration of this principle is found in the Old Testament. Though his uncle Laban deceived and cheated Jacob over and over, Jacob continually showed him love and respect. The story begins with Jacob fleeing from Esau to his uncle Laban's household. When Jacob arrived at a well, he met some men, and inquired as to whether they knew Laban or not. While Jacob was speaking, Rachel, who was one of Laban's two daughters and a shepherdess, approached the well to water her flock of sheep.

It was certainly love at first sight for both of them. Since, the well had a large stone over it, he ran up, moved the stone, identified himself as a relative of her father Laban, and kissed her on the cheek. He was so overwhelmed by her that he began to weep. She ran and told her father. Once Laban heard the news, he ran out to greet Jacob and invited him in to stay. For a month, Jacob enjoyed his hospitality, until one day, his uncle Laban made a proposition. He was a shrewd man and knew what to do.

He wanted to pay Jacob for the work that he was doing for him. Jacob immediately responded with his own offer. He desired only one wage, and it was the hand of Rachel in marriage. So, Jacob offered his uncle seven years of service for Rachel. Jacob was in love! Moses wrote that the seven years was as a few days because of his love for her. When the time finally came, Jacob came for his promised bride and consummated the marriage with his bride Rachel. By ancient custom, the bride would be veiled until the marriage was consummated. When morning came, Jacob discovered his uncle was really a treacherous man. He had replaced Rachel with his older daughter Leah. Since the bride had remained veiled, Laban's trickery could be accomplished.

When Jacob awoke, he confronted his uncle concerning this terrible deceit. He had worked seven years, as was their agreement, and he should have received Rachel as his only wife. Unfortunately, in that culture the father had ultimate authority so Jacob could not just run away with her. Laban's response was clear and direct. In his family, the older daughter was to be married off first. If Jacob would complete the marriage week with Leah, he could then have his permission to marry Rachel. Once he completed Rachel's marriage week, he had to work another seven years. As Jacob worked, his family grew.

Eventually, Jacob had eleven sons and one daughter, and God told him it was time for him to return to his father's homeland. Laban insisted he stay and claimed that he had divined that it was the Lord's will. To convince him, his uncle offered him whatever wages he desired to stay. Jacob responded by explaining that all he had done for Laban had prospered, but he wasn't building a financial base for his own family. Laban knew he depended on Jacob's wisdom and relationship to God for his prosperity and kept insisting that Jacob take the deal.

So, Jacob conceded and trusted his uncle once again. For his wages, Jacob would take all of Laban's speckled, spotted, and streaked sheep and goats to raise up his own flocks. In this way his flocks would be clearly distinguishable from from Laban's. If any other sheep or goats were found among his flocks, his uncle Laban could consider them stolen. The two agreed and his uncle Laban separated the designated animals from his own flocks and had his men drive them a journey of three days away. This way, Jacob's new flocks could not mate with the other ones. Laban thought Jacob would have to begin with such a small number that it would guarantee Jacob's service for years to come. Since Jacob was a believer and righteous man, he did not retaliate against his uncle. God had already told Jacob in a dream that he would bless all those animals.

As Laban saw God blessing Jacob's flocks, he decided to alter the terms of their arrangement ten different times. If the Lord God multiplied one kind of animal, Laban would take them. Then God would bless another kind. His uncle would return them and take the others. This happened over and over again. God kept blessing Jacob's flocks over Laban's. As a result, God had avenged Jacob, rather than him doing it on his own. The more obstinate Laban became, the more Jacob responded in love. After six short years, Jacob's flocks were enormous. This allowed him to add many servants, camels, and donkeys to his wealth. Once the sons of Laban, Jacob's cousins, saw what was happening, they became very jealous. Since Jacob's original flocks came from their father's flocks, they claimed that he had stolen the animals from their father and prospered off him. They ignored the fourteen years he had worked for their sisters. Once Jacob began to hear the grumblings, he decided it was time to depart or things could get rough. He determined not to notify Laban, so he could avoid his wrath. Once again, the Lord told Jacob to go back to his homeland, where God's promise of prosperity lied.

When Laban found out, he pursued after Jacob and then confronted his nephew. The uncle refused to fully reconcile the way God would desire and instead asked for a treaty. He did not want a future war between their clans. Yet, Jacob loved him, in spite of this. Had Laban reconciled with Jacob in a holy way, their relationship could have been restored to perhaps an even greater level. Jacob made peace as best he could. Sometimes, this is all we are able to do as believers. So, if someone will not reconcile the relationship, we should at least love them on whatever level we can, even if they desire to be an enemy.

A Modern Anecdote

Friendships are often easy to begin but very difficult to end. We seem to know intuitively how to start a variety of relationships but seem to stumble around when we need to get out of one of them. When this happens, there sometimes can be horrible consequences. A woman named Joyce, who did not end a relationship well, made an appointment with me. She described herself as a happy, upbeat, and positive person. She did not like being around negative people ever. This made her happiness fade away and darkness come.

This depressed her, so she avoided people like that. She had just broken up with a friend and told me the story. They were cashiers in a supermarket. It all started when a dog ran quickly into the store. It was a little thing which obviously was hungry and had nowhere to go. The two of them chased the dog all over the store until she caught him. The other ran into the break room to get a paper bowl and took some food from her lunch, and they took it outside and fed him. They discovered that they were both dog lovers and were happy they had found someone with a common interest. They discovered that they both dog lovers and were happy that a common interest between them had been found. Both were dog lovers what could make them happier than this?

While the dog was feeding, they got into a conversation about their dogs and decided to meet the next night at the neighborhood dog run. The two dogs got along so well that they decided to become friends. At first, the conversations were always about dogs and how to care for them, what great companions they made, and where the dogs should be taken for fun. Eventually that conversation was exhausted, and it turned to other topics. When discussing every other topic, her new friend seemed to have a negative comment. She didn't really like her job, the weather was miserable, and the city they lived in had too much crime. The government was overtaxing her, her mechanic was trying to cheat her, and her cell phone service was deplorable. Suddenly, Joyce realized she was in the presence of a negative person.

As with the others, Joyce's joy was departing, and a dark mood had arrived. Immediately and without explanation, Joyce stopped seeing the woman. She did not know how to "break up" with her and so simply avoided her whenever possible. If they had a shift together, she acted distracted and busy. If the woman called, Joyce would refuse to answer the phone. First, the woman responded by making snide remarks to customers and employees about Joyce. Though they did not know who she was talking about, Joyce knew. Next, this woman would interrupt her conversations in the break room with an opposite opinion no matter what it was. Her former friend handled the store birthday celebrations, and when it was Joyce's birthday, she had suddenly written the wrong date on her calendar. So, there was absolutely no cake or decorations to celebrate in the break room. Finally, it came to a head when they found themselves in the break room alone. The bitter woman glared at her, but Joyce would not even look up for a moment.

Eventually, the woman remarked, "What's your problem with me anyway?" Joyce could not respond. She got up and walked out of the room. Joyce had been so depressed about the whole affair that she came to see me. She seriously did not know what to do. I explained to Joyce that she had not taken the responsibility God had given her; instead, she should have gently confronted the woman. When people do not know why others reject them, they will usually fill in the blanks from their own pasts. Perhaps, she had been terribly rejected by a parent, sibling, or husband. This would only confirm in her mind something that was not true. She would become just like them, even though she is like Christ.

First, Joyce told the Lord God how sorry she was for not following His law. She should have confronted the woman and not have treated her so poorly. Then, Joyce went to the woman to make peace with her. She apologized for ignoring her, and then gently confronted her. The woman's response was complete and total disbelief. She screamed loudly, "I am not a negative person!" and stormed out. When she returned, I told her she was not responsible for the other's reaction, but she was to pray and love the obstinate. Every chance she got she should show the woman love in the ways outlined in this chapter, and let the Lord do the rest. It took some time for the relationship to be reconciled, but it finally happened. Then, the two women developed a solid work relationship.

Chapter 7

Battle and Rely

I am sure, it has become quite obvious that this process of conflict resolution is a challenge on many levels. There may be times where we may take several steps forward and then fall backward. The reason for this is that these steps are divine acts. Our Father is asking us in the name of His Son and through the power of the Holy Spirit to engage in pure supernatural thoughts, words, and actions. These cannot be accomplished in our humanity. This process of reconciliation will require time, a battle, and supernatural strength.

A Typical Scenario

Have you ever had or heard a conversation with a spouse, parent, or friend about their sister that went something like this? "Wow! I just finished talking to my mother and found out my sister has been bad-mouthing me to everyone in the family. Do you remember last year when I ran into that fence with my sister's car? Then we got into a disagreement about how much it should cost to repair and didn't speak to each other for two weeks. After we worked things out, I told her I didn't want it blabbed to everyone in the family. Now, for no apparent reason, she has decided to start talking about it. She blames the whole incident on me. I have had it with her. I'm finished. It's over. She is dead to me!"

Though this is an imaginary scenario, it illustrates the fact that there might be times where we really struggle within ourselves to resolve our disputes and make peace with others. Often, Christians have the belief that if believers were truly spiritual, they would be able to fully resolve conflicts with anybody, about anything, and at any time. This conflict resolution process should come immediately and completely for the mature saint. When it doesn't happen, these people are immature, carnal, and fleshly. This concept could not be further from the truth. The conflict resolution process may take some time to complete at any spiritual maturity level.

A Scriptural Principle

In this chapter, we discuss a biblical truth that will help us avoid putting pressure on ourselves or others involved as we proceed through the reconciliation process. The seventh principle is "we must know that reconciliation will require supernatural strength, time, and a battle." We have seen that to restore a relationship requires a divine act on God's part in our lives. This is something that God does. It comes from His character, His power, and His Spirit. In Psalm 86:5, David cried out, "For you, Lord, are good, and ready to forgive; abundant in loving kindness to all those who call on you." The Lord God's forgiveness and desire to reconcile which pours out of His loving kindness is a supernatural characteristic of deity. This truth means that we may need to be patient with ourselves and others as we all struggle with behaving in a divine and supernatural way.

A Biblical Explanation

How do we build up this divinely powerful, supernatural strength to win this battle? Though not as often utilized by believers as they should be, it is primarily through God's two strength builders: the Bible and prayer. Paul explains the power of God's Word in his letter to the Thessalonian church. Paul had only been in Thessalonica for a very short time, but the gospel (God's Word) had a mighty, explosive, supernatural, and powerful effect on these believers. In 1 Thessalonians 1:5, the apostle declares, "And that our Good News came to you not in word only, but also in power, and in the Holy Spirit." The gospel came in word (this is what we read), and in power (as we live it), and in the Holy Spirit (as He enables us). The Greek word which is translated "power," is the Greek root word from which we get our English word "dynamite." It speaks of explosive and mighty power. And this power is the power of deity; it is supernatural power. When we read the Word and gain knowledge of God and how he desires us to act, we gain the power to live it out through His Spirit.

Before, during, and after this study of God's Holy Word, we should pray for His strength and a willing heart to obey. We should ask God for this same strength and heart for the others involved. Paul exhorted the church at Thessalonica to "pray without ceasing" (1 Thessalonians 5:17). As spiritual strength is gained, we must put on the full armor of God to battle three formidable enemies which we have discussed throughout this series: the flesh, the world system, and the Devil.

This armor is discussed by the apostle Paul in Ephesians 6:10-20. Paul begins with the supernatural strength needed to put on the armor. In Ephesians 6:10, he asserts, "Finally, be strong in the Lord and in the strength of His might." Then in Ephesians 6:16, the apostle actually describes the battle as extinguishing the "flaming arrows of the evil one." The picture is of archers shooting fiery arrows into a crowd of warriors to maim or kill them. Their hope was for them to become confused, disunified, and retreat from the battle. At times, the arrows are coming so quickly that we can hardly catch our breath. We stagger spiritually and eventually may fall into the sins of a hardened heart. Our unwillingness to reconcile can produce bitterness, anger, despair, slander, a desire for revenge, and many other evils.

Each piece of armor is critical to the battle we must face. Let us look at the defensive armor first from top to bottom. Paul mentions the "helmet of salvation." The soldier had to put his helmet on to protect his head. A blow to the head by a sword would kill him instantly. This refers to the person being saved and acknowledging he or she must act as if they are saved. To apply this to our context, we must be saved to forgive. We must be true Christians and understand that true Christians forgive. Those who have not received Jesus as Savior and Lord may angry and bitter and act on it, but that is not the way of the believer.

Second, the breastplate of righteousness should be taken up. This is generally the confession of sin and the pursuit after righteous deeds. In 2 Timothy 2:22, Paul tells Timothy, "Flee from youthful lusts; but pursue righteousness, faith, love, and peace with those who call on the Lord out of a pure heart." In our context, they must pursue what is right in the reconciliation process. A "right" response would be the confession of our sins to God and to the other person. Then, they ought to pursue the "right" course of action to rebuild what was destroyed. Also, we should be engaged in general righteous living. It will be much easier to reconcile than if we are involved in sinful living.

Third, soldier saints are to "gird their loins with truth" in their battle. The Roman soldier had to roll his long garb up and tighten it with a belt in order to fight. This does not refer to honesty but the knowledge and understanding of God's truth in the Scriptures. The warrior must know the truth of God and not be fooled by Satan's lies (John 8:44). In our context, they must know the truth well enough to be able to discern at every point what the Truth says about the issue and what is the proper biblical response. We must discern the lies and know how to handle them.

Fourth, God's warrior must have the appropriate shoes. His feet must be "shod with the gospel of peace." The Roman soldier wore a cleat-like shoe into battle, so he could never lose his footing. These special shoes had spikes under them to entrench the feet into the ground for balance in the time of battle. These are similar to the cleats a football player wears on the football field. They utilize them for much needed traction and balance. This refers to the full understanding of the gospel and the regular and consistent sharing of it. When one is interested in winning people to Christ, they are much more sensitive to their words and actions in their different relationships. They are more cognizant of the importance of being an example of what a person looks like and how they act when Christ is in their lives. They will go out of their way not to offend them as they are attempting to share the gospel with the person they may have the issue with.

Fifth, these mighty warriors are to defend themselves with "the shield of faith." These shields were big enough to hide behind and to take the blows of a sword. They were covered with pitch and could immediately extinguish the flaming arrows of an enemy archer.

We must battle with a grounded, steadfast faith believing in God's Word and His power to fulfill all of its principles. In our context, we disregard our feelings or experiences and follow God's laws in reconciliation. We believe that if we follow God's blueprint, we will be successful in restoring the relationship or obeying the will of God if He has different plans. If the Lord says to forgive, then we believe Him and forgive. We do not wait for our feelings to catch up and match our obedience. We do not depend on the experience we are having in the relationship. If we are afraid the person may not respond, we should begin the process anyway. We ought to repent and let God work in the other person's life. Even when we do not emotionally "feel" like it, we will build bridges to restore the relationship by faith.

There are also two offensive weapons for our numerous spiritual battles. The first is "the sword of the spirit, which is the Word of God." The Greek word translated "Word" means specific utterances of the Word. In 1 Peter 1:25, Peter uses the same word when he writes, "'But the Word of the Lord endures forever.' And this is the word which was preached to you." This refers to the specific preached words of the Scriptures. A warrior is always attacking with his sword.

In our context, we stand against our flesh and say in our minds that we are saved (helmet of salvation) and now live for God. He desires for us to repent and ask for forgiveness or forgive. This is what God desires, and we will obey. The flesh will counter with all kinds of reasons why we shouldn't act like God. We must then decide who we will follow: God or our flesh, our new master or old master.

The second offensive weapon is prayer. I like to call it the spear of prayer, though Paul simply adds it in at the end. In Ephesians 6:18-20, he implored, "With all prayer and petition pray at all times in the Spirit, and with this in view, be on the alert with all perseverance and petition for all the saints, and pray on my behalf, that utterance may be given to me in the opening of my mouth, to make known with boldness the mystery of the gospel." In the midst of the battle the warrior is communicating constantly with the commander and with the other warriors in battle. Each is supporting the other as they follow the commands of their leader. When we need help, we ask for it, when others need help, they ask us. In 1 Thessalonians 5:25, in the midst of the raging battle with the forces of evil, Paul cried out, "Brothers, pray for us."

An Ancient Portrait

An example of this battle against sin, though ultimately lost, is the story of Cain and Abel in Genesis four. Here we see the battle up close. Once Adam and Eve sinned, they were basically thrown out of the garden. Cain was the first one born out of the union between these two people. After his brother Abel was born, we are not told much about the two brothers, except that Abel kept flocks and his brother Cain farmed. By this time, Adam had taught his children that God desired a blood sacrifice in order to properly worship Him. When it came time to bring an offering to the Lord, Cain brought an offering of his crops. He brought the first fruits. That made perfect sense because Cain was a farmer. Abel brought the first of his flocks and their fat portions. That made sense because Abel was a shepherd and cattleman.

Yet, the Lord had no regard for Cain's offering. Why? In Hebrews 11:4, the author illuminates the situation, "By faith, Abel offered to God a more excellent sacrifice than Cain, through which he had testimony given to him that he was righteous, God testifying with respect to his gifts; and through it he, being dead, still speaks." When God accepted the gifts of Abel, He was confirming the true faith that Abel had toward Him. Abel's true faith produced a righteous life which brought the recognition of his sin and the need for repentance. The true believer then acts in accordance with how God desires him to present himself before the Lord. In this case, it was through a blood sacrifice. Cain, on the other hand, was an unrighteous man coming to the Lord in his own "good" works. In 1 John 3:12, John gets to the heart of Cain's problem, when he says, "Unlike Cain, who was of the evil one, and killed his brother." Cain was of the Devil. He did not follow God in faith. Instead, he followed the Devil and did as the Devil did. Then the apostle adds, "Why did he kill him? Because his deeds were evil, and his brother's righteous." Cain did bring the best of what he grew, but it was not what God desired. It was what Cain desired.

We cannot get to God in our own way! Cain attempted to get to God through his own good deeds. When the offerings came, God was pleased with Abel's faith-based offering, but would not accept Cain's prideful rebellious offering. So, Cain immediately became angry because his younger brother was righteous, and he was evil. Wickedness hates righteousness, so Cain became sullen, and it could be clearly seen. Then, the Lord spoke to Cain and asked him why he was so angry and why had his face become so sullen. Here the Lord God provided a chance for Cain to repent of his anger and the improper sacrifice. Then, he could offer the proper one. All he had to do was, repent, believe, and demonstrate that belief through the offering of a blood sacrifice.

God told Cain to go and do well; then, he would not feel anger but joy. The solution was so simple. Don't be angry at your brother because I wouldn't accept the sacrifice, simply go and get the proper sacrifice. Then He issues a warning. He tells him sin is crouching at the door and desires to take him over. Sin like a hungry animal is crouching and waiting for the opportune time to pounce on him and take control of him. He urged Cain to master it. He must get control of his flesh, his anger, and his rebellion. Here is the battle with the flesh. He provides a choice that we all have. Do we want to do well or not? The real issue is who is going to be our master? Sin or God? Will it be our desires or God's desires? Unfortunately, sin's desires overcame evil Cain but should not with us.

Then Cain lured his brother into a field where no one was around. While they were alone, Cain killed his brother. After this, the Lord asked Cain where his brother was. Of course, the Lord God knew, but He was providing an opportunity for Cain to repent once again. Cain should have said, "He's gone Lord, and I killed him. God, I am so sorry." Instead, he sarcastically responded, "I do not know. Am I my brother's keeper?" Then the Lord cried, "What have you done?" This was an opportunity to repent. Then God told him that Abel's blood was crying out to Him. God knew exactly what he had done, and Abel's blood was the real witness of his murder. In His justice, God curses the ground which Cain depended upon for his sustenance. Cain took Adam's son away, now God was going to take Cain's livelihood away. The ground will be cursed because it bears the body of Abel. Since the ground would no longer grow crops for him, he would have to wander upon the earth. He would become nothing more than a vagrant.

He knew that once people found out about his curse, they would kill him. In God's mercy, He placed a mark on his forehead and proclaimed that whoever killed Cain, His vengeance would be on him sevenfold. Why? God decides the sentence alone, not an individual. This would be both a mark of disdain and protection. Notice, he did not ask for forgiveness nor seek peace. So, Moses writes that Cain went out from the presence of the Lord and settled in the land of Nod. What a great example of the battle with the flesh, even though Cain lost that battle.

Cain had God's presence to encourage him to stand against the flesh. We have God's Holy Spirit inside of us. God spoke to him, and he spoke to God. God speaks to us through His Word, and we speak to Him through prayer. In our context of reconciliation, we need to repent of our sinful actions which lead to relationship issues. Then, we pray and read the Word to acquire the power we need to restore the relationship using the armor of God. We must put on the armor so we will win the battle against the flesh, the world, and the Devil. They do not want relationships to be whole but broken or destroyed. Christians need to go and reconcile their relationships through God's strength. Though this may require a battle, it is God's blueprint.

A Modern Anecdote

Christians are required to reconcile all their relationships, including those of co-workers. This is often neglected, yet problems with people we work with abound. Everyone has a story about a problem with their boss or fellow worker. One such man walked into my office slumped over in defeat and brokenness. He was a new teacher at his school, and He had tried with great effort and difficulty to solve a problem that he had with the fifth-grade teacher next door. It all started with a red ball. The rule in the elementary school was that only yellow balls could be used for kick ball because they were thicker and could endure the physical abuse. Because they were thinner, the red balls were to be used for playing catch, foursquare, and handball. When he came to the school the classroom had no yellow balls. He was very concerned about his students being able to play kickball. This had been his favorite game in grade school. He wanted to use it for P.E. and teach the children some cool tricks he had learned.

When he had ordered the yellow balls from the district, he discovered that they were on back order. He couldn't find one yellow ball to use in the school. Only four classrooms had them, and they didn't want them kicked over the fence, lost, or popped. So, they would not loan them out to this new teacher. The man ordered several red balls. Since there were no yellow balls, his class would use the red ball to kick. He did not think much of it because he used his class money. It seemed like such a mundane thing to him, and he felt that rules were to serve people, not for people to serve the rules.

Nobody said anything as his class played kickball at his P.E. period. One day, his students begged him to allow them to use the red ball at recess because there were no yellow balls to kick during that time. He thought that this should not be a problem, so he allowed it.

When recess was over, the teacher next door stomped up to him while both classes were lined up next to each other and yelled, "Mr. Jackson [not his real name], your class was kicking a red ball. That is against the rules." With complete surprise, he calmly responded by explaining the problem and his solution." She starred at him and shouted, "Rules are rules. They must be followed by everyone." This made him angry, so he shouted his response that rules are meant to serve people and not the other way around. She glared at him and then shouted at her class to follow her; then, they went off to her classroom. It wasn't long before this man was somewhat of a celebrity in the school because he was kind, funny, an enthusiastic teacher, and interested in school being a place the children wanted to be.

This only added fuel to the hot fire. A few weeks later, he discovered that she was constantly complaining about him to the principal, back-biting him in the lunchroom, and criticizing him to her class. This had to stop. He stormed into her empty classroom one day after school and blasted, "Why don't you get a life and leave me alone." An argument ensued, and he marched out. This continued for over three months. She would complain, back-bite, and criticize him; then, he would storm in and blast her. Until one day, he was reading the Scriptures at home and read several passages on reconciling as God has reconciled with us. The Holy Spirit convicted him at that moment so powerfully that he felt a huge weight was now leaning on his shoulders. He did not know exactly what to do. He had found himself in a vicious cycle and did not know how to get out of it.

I explained to him that he had to reconcile with her. He had to go and apologize for his part in the situation and resolve the conflict. Then he had to build a relationship that would honor the Lord. He told me that he didn't think he could do it. I explained that it would take spiritual strength, time, and a battle with his flesh. I described the armor of God and explained how to put it on with her. It took him three weeks of prayer and study of the Word to approach her. The first encounter turned once again into an argument. The second encounter he opened the door of her classroom, shook his head, and walked out. The third time, he had a pleasant conversation but couldn't get himself to apologize. Finally, the man had enough spiritual strength to walk into her classroom and apologize. She sat silent. Over several months, he followed God's blueprint of reconciliation. The result was the building of a God-honoring work relationship with her.

Chapter 8

Act Like Him

If you made it to the end of this book, then you possess all the tools needed to make a relationship last for a lifetime. Wait a minute, isn't that what we hope relationships will do? Don't we wish for them to last a lifetime? Isn't that what the Lord desires for marriage relationships to do? Doesn't our Father command that they have lifelong covenants? Why aren't they? To possess the tools is not enough, both people must use them. For this to really happen, only one more issue needs discussion. Will you do it? Many people leave my office with exactly the same bag of tools to repair their relationships and yet some crash and burn and others go on to live very happy fulfilled lives in their marriages, families, friendships, churches, and other various partnerships. What makes the difference? It is the motivation and desire to obey God. What makes one person utilize the tools I have given them from God's Word and the other not? It is the genuine willingness to follow the Lord, the serious commitment to submit to all His commands, and the absolute desire to live like Him and His Son through His Holy Spirit.

A Typical Scenario

Have you ever had or heard a conversation with a spouse to a friend that went something like this? "No, it is over. I am done with this marriage. Yes, I went to counseling with him and I know what to do, but I don't want to do it. Too many things have happened. (Friend responds.) I do not care what the Bible says. I am extremely unhappy, and that's all there is to it (Friend responds.) Yes, I have seen some change, but it is too little, too late. I went to another counselor, and she told me that I should look out for my own emotional well-being, so I am. (Friend responds.) The children will be fine. Divorce is very common today. They will still get to see their father every other weekend and holidays. (Friend responds.) Yes, they cried and cried, but I told them that they would be much happier if mommy and daddy weren't fighting all the time. (Friend responds.) What about my church's reaction? If they give me any trouble, I will just find another one. When I walk into the next one, I will just tell them I'm divorced."

This scenario is typical of many people as they rationalize their destruction of their lifelong covenant. Many of these people do have deep wounds from their relationships, but they can be restored using the tools from Scripture. If both are Christians, their main desire for restoration should be to live like their Lord. If God had abandoned us, we would be on our way to hell. Yet, God has made a lifelong covenant with us; He constantly seeks reconciliation with us no matter what we do. Then, God desires us to do the same to others.

A Scriptural Principle

We come to the final principle involving the motivation for reconciling. Let's face it, relationships are difficult at times because not only do we make numerous mistakes, but so do others. It is hard to seek peace. We must have some serious reasons for engaging in the restoration process because it is so easy to give up and start over. This brings us to principle eight which is "we must resolve conflicts because we must act just like God." This may seem simple or even a bit strange as a motivation because it is not geared toward our betterment or the fulfillment of our needs. It involves the honoring and glorifying of God. Our motivation is all about the Lord God and only secondarily about us. It is the opposite of the world's desire to revolve itself around the individual and their needs. We want everything to be about us - our needs, our wants, our lives. This is not how the Lord God works. The motivation of "acting like Him" is deeply spiritual and is what the Spirit thrives on in a believer's life.

A Biblical Explanation

To comprehend why we as Christians must forgive and reconcile all broken relationships, we must understand the very person of the God who sent His only Son to die in order to forgive and reconcile the broken relationship we had with Him. We must understand His character that brought forth the love, grace, and mercy demonstrated in the work that had to be accomplished to restore our relationship that we had with Him in the garden. This knowledge will bring the desire to utilize these tools that have been presented in this book from the Scriptures and will become the driving force in our own forgiveness and reconciliation with others.

Since this is the ultimate reason which drives Christians to forgive and reconcile with others, we must discuss this carefully providing the Spirit with the truth that is needed to unleash His power in our lives to forgive and reconcile. The supernatural work that the Lord asks us as His children to accomplish in our relationships with one another and those outside the faith involve the gracious attitudes and actions which He Himself showed us. We must feel compelled to demonstrate the same to others. The old adage becomes all too true with the Godhead: "Like Father, like Son (Jesus)." Then, perhaps we might continue, "Like Son (Jesus), like sons (us)." As God's supernatural offspring, we act like Him.

We must behave like our God. In Daniel 9:9, the prophet boldly declares, "To the Lord our God belong mercies and forgiveness." The source of all our forgiveness comes out of the loving, gracious, and merciful character of God and there is no Being like Him. Over and over in the Scriptures, we are commanded to think and act like our Father. In 1 Peter 1:15-16, the apostle Peter exclaims, "But just as he who called you is holy, you yourselves also be holy in all of your behavior." Just as our Father is holy in His behavior, His children are to be in theirs. Then the apostle quotes an extremely familiar Old Testament passage to the Jewish people, "Because it is written, "You shall be holy; for I am holy." This important Greek word translated "holy" means "set apart." We might think of it as "separate from or wholly different from" men.

Therefore, our Lord expects His children to be "set apart, separate, or wholly different" from the world around them in their thinking, feeling, and behaving. This is not easy. It requires much time in the Word, prayer, and spending time among believers who think, feel, and act this same way. One of these holy ways of God is forgiveness. Though the world may harbor bitterness, we forgive. Though the world might demand a whole set of actions to forgive, we do not. Since the Lord forgives us, we act in the same manner and forgive others. We behave wholly differently, and this demonstrates, we are the true children of God.

We know that forgiving someone or humbly asking for forgiveness is difficult to do. When this struggle begins, then we must remember that we are to be wholly different from the world and be holy like Him which involves forgiving. He forgave us and we forgive others. He forgave us and we ask for forgiveness of others.

One last truth must be discussed. One of the barriers to forgiving others is feeling victimized by people. We do not want to forgive because we feel that we are victims of others. This creates in us an anger that is difficult to remove. This stands in the way of reconciliation. Yet, we should recognize God's sovereignty in allowing the sinful actions we are to forgive. We must accept God's reign and control over us and the world that affects us.

When people sin against us, they must be allowed to do that by God. Job said it best when he told his wife in Job 2:10, "But he said to her, 'You speak as one of the foolish women speaks. Shall we indeed accept good from God and not adversity?' In all this, Job did not sin with his lips." Note that comment by Job was true. He did not sin by telling a falsehood with His lips. Yet, it was Satan that hurt, maimed, and "victimized" him. Job didn't view the situation this way. He recognized the reign of God over the whole earth and accepted it. Satan had to ask permission.

When people sin against us, it must be allowed by God. They cannot victimize us. They can become instruments of God's work in our lives as the Lord brings trials among us, but nobody sneaks by Him to hurt or harm us. This is such a critical point. Since God is in charge, we are not anyone's victim. This was so clearly indicated by Jesus at his arrest. Peter decided to intervene and drew his sword to fight the crowd and cut the ear off one of the servants. Jesus told him to put his sword down.

Then in Matthew 26:53, He asks Peter, "Do you think that I cannot appeal to My Father, and He will at once put at My disposal more than twelve legions of angels?" God was in control. He always had been from the moment Jesus was born, and He was no victim. The Father had allowed them to act. He could intervene at any time. When someone sins against us, God has allowed it. We see this when Jesus stood before the great Pontius Pilate. In John 19:10, John records, "Pilate therefore said to Him, 'You do not speak to me? Do you not know I have authority to release You and I have authority to crucify you?'" Pontius Pilate thought that he was in control and had the authority to decide whether Jesus would live or die but was not. In John 11:11, Jesus sets him straight, "Jesus answered him, 'You would have no authority over Me, unless it had been given you from above.'" He was a powerful man, but he couldn't do anything without the approval of God. We must trust the Lord God in His sovereignty and know that we are never victims.

An Ancient Portrait

Two great examples of this principle are the Lord Jesus as He patterned His forgiveness and desire for reconciliation after the Father and then Stephen as He followed his Lord in the same way. Christ desired reconciliation with those who were the participants in His crucifixion and asked the Father to forgive them. In Luke 23:34, the Lord was hanging on the cross, dripping with blood from the crown of thorns and the nails in his hands and feet. In His excruciating pain from the tortures and violent beatings, agonizing in the slow dying process, humiliated from the mocking of all the people, He cried out loudly to His Father God to forgive those ignorant persecutors. Who were they?

The Romans, who were doing all the dirty work the Jews could not do, did not realize that they were really crucifying the ultimate King of Kings and Lord of Lords. The common Jews, who were standing around the cross throwing insults at the Lord, could not fully understand that their longed-for Messiah, was hanging from that cursed tree. The frightened disciples who had scattered from the mob could not fully comprehend that their great moment of victory in salvation had not been lost in that dying man. Instead, it was about to be completed when the price was paid, and Christ had risen from the dead. Even, many of the rulers, who were caught up in their self-righteous pride, could not perceive that the veil of the temple was about to be split into two. The lamb would be sacrificed, and the new eternal high priest would enter the Holy of Holies to represent them before the Father in heaven.

In the midst of his deep pain, Christ knowing all of this, looked down with great compassion, and cried out for the Father's forgiveness. Christians know through their study of the Scriptures that the prayer could only be fulfilled if all of these ignorant, hardhearted persecutors and enemies of the cross received the soon to be risen Son of God as Savior and Lord. Yet, implied in the merciful cry to His Father, is a God who became truly man, and as man forgave His persecutors, tormentors, and scoffers.

Then, near the moment of His own death, He forgave the repentant thief hanging next to him as he turned to the Lord for salvation. In Luke 23:35-43, the Lord Jesus was hanging on the cross while two others were being crucified next to him. These were real criminals on either side of Him, not a God-Man. They too were hurling the same kind of abuse as those below. Like the people all around Jesus, these two thieves were hurling insults at Jesus for claiming to be the Christ, the chosen one of God, the long-awaited Messiah, and the one who fulfilled all the prophecies from ancient days. Yet, he could not save Himself from such a despicable fate.

Suddenly, one of the two thieves grew silent as the other continued his mockery. Then he prepared himself for death and considered his wicked life. He saw before his own eyes a perfect and innocent man. He must have taken a moment to ponder the very words he had spoken about Jesus' deity, the sign of His dignity, and the belief of His disciples in His divinity that was on display before them. In that moment, through the power of the Holy Spirit his blinders from Satan fell off, his prideful rationalizations for his own sins tumbled from his broken flesh, then he repented and believed. He grew sorrowful and mournful for his sins and believed that Jesus was indeed who He claimed to be. He was the Son of the living God and Savior of the world. Then deep within his heart he submitted to His Lordship.

Moments before this, the thief had cursed and criticized Jesus, now he turned toward the other thief and robber and cried out for him to cease from his abusive words. The thief declared that they deserved everything they had gotten, but Jesus had done nothing wicked His whole life. Through this, the thief affirmed his new belief that Jesus was a righteous and holy God. Before Him, these two criminals were utterly without merit.

He questioned the other condemned outlaw as to whether he feared God. Judgment was coming; it was at their door. The physical life was draining from their bodies, and their eternal spirits would face an almighty God. As Jews, they knew the law and would have a greater judgment than the Gentiles. They had lived sin filled lives and now had been blaspheming God's anointed Messiah. Their condemnation would be unimaginable. The other thief must stop.

Then he turned toward Jesus Christ and asked the saving question that demonstrated all that the Holy Spirit had done in His life. He asked the Lord to remember him when He came into His Kingdom. There it was: a recognition of who Jesus was and what He was doing on the cross that day. He was not saving Himself so He could save others and the thief desperately desired that deliverance. So, at the moment of his death, the man cried out for forgiveness and salvation. When Jesus gives up His spirit and enters the abode of His Father will He please remember this repentant criminal and bring his unworthy soul into His heaven. As the life was slowly pouring out of Him, Jesus looked at the man and declared on that very day this repentant sinner and now true saint would be with Him in paradise. Peace between God and that man had come.

Later, in Acts 7:54-59, Stephen, a disciple, preached before the Sanhedrin and indicted them for their hypocritical sin. They responded by rushing him, dragging him out of the city, and stoning him to death. In verse 60, Luke records Stephen's Christ-like and God the Father-like response, "He kneeled down, and cried with a loud voice, 'Lord, don't hold this sin against them!' When he had said this, he fell asleep." In his final words in Acts 7:60, Stephen took up Jesus Christ's compassionate mantle and begged God for their forgiveness. Stephen sought peace with them.

All Christians are compelled by their Lord and Savior to forgive anyone and everyone, believer or unbeliever, friend or foe, brother or acquaintance, and persecutor or supporter for any and all transgressions! This leads to reconciliation and is not human; instead, it is a supernatural phenomenon. In the gospels and epistles, it clearly states that saints are to forgive both other believers and unbelievers. Christians are to seek peace with others. Why? Saints are to act like their Father and Lord who also forgives everything at salvation eternally and continually afterward relationally. Though this is not the only step in reconciliation, it is the critical one. We must desire to forgive the sins of our enemies.

A Modern Anecdote

A medical doctor entered my office with a great sense of frustration concerning a colleague of his. They had been best friends for as long as he could remember. His parents had moved to another state when he was in middle school, and they had kept in touch for years. Both had entered medical school and had specialized in pediatrics. Both ended up in a large town near my office. Once they had both settled into their practices, they took up where they had left off. They played golf together, attended numerous conferences and trainings, and even consulted on each other's patients. Their families attended the same church and went on vacation every year together and their wives and kids had become very close.

The problem began when his dearest friend received an award from a prestigious medical association. This made him feel uneasy, but he brushed it off. Then his friend was selected as one of the top ten physicians by a magazine in their city. Now he knew that his friend was an excellent pediatrician, but this was simply too much. Why wasn't he selected? Once his physician friend had an article in the magazine, his private practice suddenly took on a tidal wave of patients. This was too much for my counselee to bear. For the first time in his life, he experienced envy and jealousy.

This quickly brought forth deep within his heart a sense of resentment. His first response was to pretend that nothing was wrong. Then, he could not make their usual golf game. Since he had to attend the conference late, he suggested that they shouldn't share their usual room. At the conference, he did everything he could do to avoid this award-winning friend. The worst part was that his dear friend was receiving an enormous amount of attention. This only frustrated him even more and produced an anger that he also had never felt before. When vacation planning started, he suggested to his wife that they do something different this next year. She refused, and a fight ensued. When she demanded that he explain himself, he couldn't reveal his feelings. How could this man explain his envy, jealousy, resentment, and anger toward such a dear friend? Unfortunately, during the entire vacation he barely spoke to him. He always provided a wide variety of excuses which simply did not add up.

Then another emotion entered the scene: bitterness. Not toward his friend but toward God. Why had God allowed this to happen? Why was God playing favorites? He was as strong a Christian as his friend. Why does his friend get the recognition for which he had longed? When this bitterness took root, he stopped attending church, men's group, and reading the Bible and praying. Now his wife stepped in and begged him to see me. I took him to several passages in the Scriptures. We discussed how James and John asked to sit on either side of Jesus in His kingdom (Matthew 20:20-22). We perused the story of his disciples arguing over who would be greatest in His kingdom (Luke 9:46). We even studied the fact that careers and achievement are not the focus of God's attention but instead seeking first His kingdom (Matthew 6:33).

Finally, we studied the parable of the day laborers told by Jesus (Matthew 20:1-16). Some had worked a full day and others worked only an hour, God decided they would both get the same wages (heaven). God decides how He blesses, when He blesses, and who he blesses, we should be grateful for anything we are given since we truly deserve nothing. He began to realize that he was not behaving like his Father, imitating the Son, or walking in the Spirit. He was not acting "wholly separated" from those who do not know Christ. He was supposed to be holy. The Lord Jesus Christ did not seek the world's achievement but God's favor. He was to do the same. Once he realized what he had done, he had to take the next step which was to go and reconcile with his Father in heaven and his friend on earth.

Conclusion

As we conclude this book, I would like to leave us with some final thoughts about our God of reconciliation and what His Son did on the cross for us. First, if we understand the full extent of what was wrought for us on that cursed tree in order to make peace with us, it will become so much easier to do the same thing for others. Second, if you read this entire book and realized that you do not understand salvation or have never received Christ as Lord and Savior, then I would like to provide that opportunity. Please do not skip this section; it may be the most important in your life.

From all outward appearances, humans seem "good" and attempt to live decent lives. This is man's concept of himself. This is not God's concept. The Almighty's view is that people all over the world and throughout the ages sin, sin, and sin again (Romans 3:23). This is a terrible and utterly destructive condition. Yet, they have ramifications that are far worse. These sins condemn us to everlasting divine retribution.

Though described briefly in the Old Testament, the Lord Jesus Christ clearly announced and proclaimed the future punishment to come. Contrary to popular belief, Jesus did not only speak of love, grace, and mercy, He also spoke of the coming judgment for sin. He declared that the judgment of sin would be everlasting punishment in a place He called "Hell." The Lord portrayed this place as an eternal inferno (Matthew 18:8) where there would be the weeping (from the sorrow) and gnashing of teeth (from the agony and anguish of suffering) continually into eternity (Matthew 8:12; 13:42, 50; 22:13; 24:51; 25:30; Luke 13:28).

Why must people face this horrific punishment? Though God is a God of love, grace, and mercy, He is also a God of great holiness, righteousness, and justice (Psalm 89:14,18). These attributes are just as much a part of His divine nature as His love, grace, and mercy. You have broken God's law as we all have, and the penalty must be paid. This began with the first man Adam (Genesis 3:1-7). When this occurred, His love, grace, and mercy surfaced, and a provision was made. Someone else would have to take man's place and pay the penalty. Someone who had never transgressed Him, who would never deserve punishment, and would fulfill all of God's Laws, would be substituted in man's place. This was the Son of God, Jesus Christ.

As the God-Man, He would pay the penalty for our sins in His death on the cross. Once done, the Lord God made only one provision for people to appropriate what His Son had done on the cross for them. This provision is receiving Jesus Christ as Savior and Lord. Though I cannot possibly share with you this good news in the confines of this book, I would love for you to consider purchasing my book entitled, *Finding The Light: The Kingdom of Heaven and How To Enter It.* It can be found for sale on Amazon.com. It is inexpensive and contains the full gospel message for your consideration. This message is so important and extensive that it cannot adequately be contained in a few pages at the end of a book.

If you are a believer, you must go out into the world and seek peace through reconciliation as God did for us. These principles are to be lived and shared with others. You now have the tools to make your relationships last a lifetime. Go live them out and share them with others!

ABOUT THE AUTHOR

Dr. Donald Jones is currently a Christian Pastoral Counselor with thirty-eight years of experience in the fields of pastoral ministry, public education, and Christian counseling. He carries degrees and certificates from four major universities and from a variety of educational institutions. He has been a professor of Languages and Bible, a television commentator, and a featured speaker at a variety of events and seminars at churches, schools, and other organizations across the United States. He is a member in good standing of several secular and Christian professional organizations. Dr. Jones has been a published author since 1976. For further information view his website at www.donjonesphd.com.

www.ingramcontent.com/pod-product-compliance
Lightning Source LLC
LaVergne TN
LVHW011336080426
835513LV00006B/379